To Jon
Christmas - 1994

My love always,
Janelle

D1274422

My Favorite Hymns

OTHER HARPER SAN FRANCISCO BOOKS

BY NORMAN VINCENT PEALE

My Christmas Treasury

My Favorite Prayers

My Favorite Quotations

My Inspirational Favorites

My Favorite Hymns

And the Stories Behind Them

Norman Vincent Peale

A Giniger Book
published in association with

HarperSanFrancisco
A Division of HarperCollinsPublishers

Permission credits are listed on page 177 and are to be considered
a continuation of this copyright page.

MY FAVORITE HYMNS: *and the Stories Behind Them*. Copyright © 1994 by
The Peale Foundation. All rights reserved. Published in association with The K. S. Giniger
Company, Inc., 250 West 57th Street, New York, NY 10107. No part of this book may be
used or reproduced in any manner whatsoever without written permission except in the
case of brief quotations embodied in critical articles and reviews. For information address
HarperCollins Publishers, 10 East 53rd Street, New York, NY 10022.

FIRST EDITION

Library of Congress Cataloging-in-Publication Data

Peale, Norman Vincent.
    My favorite hymns and the stories behind them / Norman Vincent Peale. — 1st ed.
        p. cm.
    "A Giniger Book"—T.p. verso
    Includes indexes.
    ISBN 0–06–066463–0 (cloth : alk. paper)
    1. Hymns—History and criticism.   I. Title.
BV315.P37   1994
264'.2—dc20   94–5585
                                                                              CIP

94 95 96 97 98 ❖ HAD 10 9 8 7 6 5 4 3 2 1

This edition is printed on acid-free paper that meets the American National
Standards Institute Z39.48 Standard.

Contents

Introduction, *Norman Vincent Peale*   ix

Adams, Sarah F. • *Nearer, My God, to Thee*   1

Alexander, Cecil F. • *Jesus Calls Us*   4

Baring-Gould, Sabine • *Onward, Christian Soldiers*   7

Bates, Katharine Lee • *America the Beautiful*   10

Bennard, George • *The Old Rugged Cross*   14

Bennett, Sanford F. • *Sweet By and By*   17

Brooks, Phillips • *O Little Town of Bethlehem*   19

Caswall, Edward C. • *When Morning Gilds the Skies*   22

Jesus, the Very Thought of Thee   25

Croly, George • *Spirit of God, Descend upon My Heart*   26

CONTENTS

Crosby, Fanny • *All the Way My Saviour Leads Me* 28

Blessed Assurance 32

Dwight, Timothy • *I Love Thy Kingdom, Lord* 33

Elliott, Charlotte • *Just as I Am* 37

Faber, Frederick W. • *Faith of Our Fathers* 39

There's a Wideness in God's Mercy 41

Fawcett, John • *Blest Be the Tie That Binds* 43

Fosdick, Harry Emerson • *God of Grace* 46

Gilmore, Joseph H. • *He Leadeth Me* 48

Gladden, Washington • *O Master, Let Me Walk with Thee* 51

Havergal, Frances R. • *Take My Life* 54

Hawks, Annie S. • *I Need Thee Every Hour* 57

Heber, Reginald • *Holy, Holy, Holy* 59

Hine, Stuart K. • *How Great Thou Art* 62

Hopper, Edward • *Jesus, Saviour, Pilot Me* 64

Howe, Julia Ward • *Battle Hymn of the Republic* 66

Lathbury, Mary • *Day Is Dying in the West* 70

Break Thou the Bread of Life 72

Luther, Martin • *A Mighty Fortress Is Our God* 73

Lyte, Henry F. • *Abide with Me* 77

Martin, Civilla D. • *God Will Take Care of You* 80

Matheson, George • *O Love That Wilt Not Let Me Go* 82

Miles, C. Austin • *In the Garden* 85

Mohr, Joseph • *Silent Night, Holy Night* 88

Newton, John • *Amazing Grace* 91

Palmer, Ray • *My Faith Looks Up to Thee* 94

Perronet, Edward • *All Hail the Power of Jesus' Name* 97

Pollard, Adelaide A. • *Have Thine Own Way, Lord* 100

Prentiss, Elizabeth P. • *More Love to Thee* 103

Roberts, Daniel C. • *God of Our Fathers* 106

Scriven, Joseph • *What a Friend We Have in Jesus* 108

Sears, Edmund H. • *It Came upon the Midnight Clear* 111

Smith, Samuel F. • *My Country, 'Tis of Thee* 114

Spafford, Horatio G. • *It Is Well with My Soul* 116

Stone, Samuel J. • *The Church's One Foundation* 119

Thompson, Will L. • *Softly and Tenderly* 122

Toplady, Augustus M. • *Rock of Ages* 124

van Dyke, Henry • *Joyful, Joyful, We Adore Thee* 127

CONTENTS

Walford, William W. • *Sweet Hour of Prayer* 130

Warner, Anna B. • *Jesus Loves Me* 132

Watts, Isaac • *O God, Our Help in Ages Past* 134

Jesus Shall Reign 137 *I Sing the Mighty Power of God* 138

When I Survey the Wondrous Cross 140

Wesley, Charles • *Jesus, Lover of My Soul* 141

Christ, the Lord, Is Risen Today 146

O For a Thousand Tongues 148

Hark! the Herald Angels Sing 149

Love Divine, All Loves Excelling 152

Whittier, John Greenleaf • *Dear Lord and Father of Mankind* 154

Williams, William • *Guide Me, O Thou Great Jehovah* 157

Acknowledgments *161*

Index of Hymn Titles *163*

Index of First Lines of Hymns *167*

Topical Index of Hymns *171*

Introduction

Hymns have always been a large part of my spiritual life. I was exposed to them at an early age in the churches my father served across Ohio. Since he was a Methodist minister in the early part of the century, we moved quite often, but the hymns we sang were the same wherever we went. I am grateful to my parents for instilling them in my memory. The poetry of each hymn and its tune sing through my consciousness to this day.

Hymn singing has been a vital part of the church for several centuries. Martin Luther said, "Music is a gift and grace of God." Every period of spiritual revival throughout the years has been accompanied by new hymns and a new enthusiasm for singing them. It seems to be a way for people to express the joy of the Christian faith.

This book contains some of my favorite hymns. As you will notice when you read the following stories, hymns were written for a variety of reasons. Many grew out of personal sorrow, tragedy, or need. Others were poems expressing the truths of the Christian faith. Hymns have been written by poets, statesmen, ministers, teachers, students—both men and women, young and old. Perhaps reading this book might encourage someone today to write a new hymn reflecting God's love and transforming power.

Hymns have blessed people throughout the ages in a variety of ways. You will read about some of these blessings in this book. In my years as a minister, many people have told me that the singing of a particular hymn brought comfort or insight in the midst of a particularly difficult situation. I hope your life too will be blessed by reading the following hymns and their stories.

—Norman Vincent Peale

Publisher's note: Norman Vincent Peale completed the manuscript for this book before his death on Christmas Eve, 1993.

My Favorite Hymns

Sarah F. Adams (1805–1848)

Nearer, My God, to Thee

On April 14, 1912, the melody of a hymn played by the ship's band drifted across the icy waters of the Atlantic as the great ship *Titanic* took fifteen hundred people to their deaths. The hymn was "Nearer, My God, to Thee." On May 21, 1889, a train was caught in the rushing waters of the Johnstown, Pennsylvania, flood. In one car, which had been thrown over on its side, stood a young woman on her way to overseas missionary service. In front of a throng of people on the shore, who knew they could not rescue her, she sang a hymn as she was engulfed by the raging waters. That hymn was "Nearer, My God, to Thee." On September 19, 1901, at the funeral of President William McKinley, and at memorial services in his honor all across the country, the hymn was sung that was on his lips when he died. That hymn was "Nearer, My God, to Thee."

This hymn, so identified with tragic situations, was written in 1840 by an Englishwoman, Sarah Adams. A Unitarian most of her life, she had taken up hymn writing when failing health forced her to give up her career as an actress. One day Sarah's minister, William J. Fox, was looking for a hymn to close a sermon on

Jacob and Esau. Sarah, who was helping him compile a hymn-book at the time, decided to write one for him to use, and "Nearer, My God, to Thee" was the result.

The current tune was composed in 1856 by Lowell Mason (1792–1872), a founding father of American church music and one of our best-known hymn tune writers. He states that the melody came to him one night as he lay in bed unable to sleep. The next morning he quickly wrote it down, and with this new tune "Nearer, My God, to Thee" gained instant popularity.

This is one hymn acceptable to all faiths. It has been translated into almost every known language.

Nearer, my God, to Thee,
    Nearer to Thee,
E'en though it be a cross
    That raiseth me!
Still all my song shall be,
    Nearer, my God, to Thee;
Nearer, my God, to Thee,
    Nearer to Thee!

Though like the wanderer,
    The sun gone down,
Darkness be over me,

My rest a stone;
Yet in my dreams I'd be
    Nearer, my God, to Thee;
Nearer, my God, to Thee,
    Nearer to Thee!

There let the way appear,
    Steps unto heaven;
All that Thou sendest me,
    In mercy given;
Angels to beckon me
    Nearer, my God, to Thee;
Nearer, my God, to Thee,
    Nearer to Thee!

Then, with my waking thoughts
    Bright with Thy praise,
Out of my stony griefs
    Bethel I'll raise;
So by my woes to be
    Nearer, my God, to Thee;
Nearer, my God, to Thee,
    Nearer to Thee!

Or if, on joyful wing
    Cleaving the sky,
Sun, moon, and stars forgot,
    Upward I fly,
Still all my song shall be,
    Nearer, my God, to Thee;
Nearer, my God, to Thee,
    Nearer to Thee!

Cecil F. Alexander (1818–1895)

Jesus Calls Us

Cecil Alexander started writing poetry at an early age, but she would hide her work under the carpet for fear her stern father would disapprove. When he discovered what she was doing, he not only encouraged her work but gathered the family together every Saturday night to listen to her recite the poems she had written that week.

When Cecil married the Reverend William Alexander, she devoted herself to helping the poor and needy in their country parish. She had a special interest in helping children understand God's love, and most of her four hundred poems and hymns were written for them. In 1848 she published a children's hymnal that sold a quarter of a million copies!

Cecil Alexander also wrote many poems for her husband to use in his sermons. "Jesus Calls Us" was written for a sermon on the calling of Jesus' disciple Andrew, and William ended his sermon on Sunday, November 30, 1852, with her new poem. Not until 1887 was it published with its current tune, written by a distinguished British musician, William H. Jude (1851–1922).

One of Alexander's poems is the source of the titles of several popular books by a Yorkshire veterinarian, James Herriot. The first stanza of that poem reads:

All things bright and beautiful
All creatures great and small
All things wise and wonderful
The Lord God made them all.

Even though William Alexander became archbishop of Ireland, he stated that no matter what he personally accomplished in his life he would always be known as Cecil Alexander's husband.

Jesus calls us; o'er the tumult
Of our life's wild, restless sea,

Day by day His sweet voice soundeth,
Saying, "Christian, follow Me."

Jesus calls us from the worship
Of the vain world's golden store,
From each idol that would keep us,
Saying, "Christian, love Me more."

In our joys and in our sorrows,
Days of toil and hours of ease,
Still He calls, in cares and pleasures,
"Christian, love Me more than these."

Jesus calls us. By Thy mercies,
Saviour, may we hear Thy call,
Give our hearts to Thy obedience,
Serve and love Thee best of all.

Sabine Baring-Gould (1834–1924)

Onward, Christian Soldiers

The classic hymn "Onward, Christian Soldiers," which has seemed too militaristic to some in recent years, was written as a children's marching song. In 1864 the Sunday school of the Reverend Baring-Gould's church was participating in a festival on Whitmonday, a yearly church holiday in Great Britain. Baring-Gould wanted the children to have a song to sing as they marched from village to village, but he couldn't find anything suitable. So he sat up late into the night writing his own marching song.

First sung to a different tune, the hymn became popular when Sir Arthur Sullivan (1842–1900), best known for his collaboration with W. S. Gilbert on such operettas as *The Mikado* and *The Pirates of Penzance,* wrote the tune currently in use.

The hymn has been translated into many languages. On Sunday, May 22, 1910, in conjunction with a world Sunday school convention, this hymn was sung in more than one hundred languages and dialects in Sunday schools around the world.

Baring-Gould, the author of another favorite hymn, "Now the Day Is Over," was one of the most gifted English writers of the nineteenth century. His eighty-five books range from religion to travel, biography to folklore, theology to fiction. He has had more titles listed under his name in the catalog of the British Museum than any other author of his day. But he is best known for a simple marching song written in haste late one evening for use at a children's festival.

Onward, Christian soldiers!
  Marching as to war,
With the cross of Jesus
  Going on before.
Christ, the royal Master,
  Leads against the foe;
Forward into battle,
  See, His banners go!

Refrain
Onward, Christian soldiers!
  Marching as to war,
With the cross of Jesus
  Going on before.

Like a mighty army
  Moves the Church of God.
Brothers, we are treading

Where the saints have trod.
We are not divided;
All one body we;
One in hope and doctrine,
One in charity.

At the sign of triumph
Satan's host doth flee;
On, then, Christian soldiers,
On to victory!
Hell's foundations quiver
At the shout of praise;
Brothers, lift your voices,
Loud your anthems raise!

Onward, then, ye people!
Join our happy throng;
Blend with ours your voices
In the triumph song.
Glory, laud, and honor
Unto Christ, the King;
This thro' countless ages
Men and angels sing.

Katharine Lee Bates (1859–1929)

America the Beautiful

In the summer of 1893 a thirty-four-year-old professor of English literature at Wellesley College in Massachusetts took a trip across the country. Invited to teach a course in religious drama at Colorado College in Colorado Springs, Katharine Bates was looking forward to seeing a different part of the United States. Her first stop was the Chicago World's Fair, which had recently opened. In the Columbian Exposition she was awestruck by the beautiful white buildings housing exhibits of America's future. These buildings, called the "White City," were masterpieces of construction and beauty and would become the "alabaster cities" of her famous hymn.

As she traveled from Chicago, she passed through rich farmlands, with their fields of grain, and then came to the mountains—majestic and awe-inspiring, portraying different moods at different times of day. At the end of the summer session, she was taken to the top of Pike's Peak, where from its 14,000-foot elevation, she looked out over the mountains and plains below and at the vast sky above. Standing on that spot, the lines of the first verse of "America the Beautiful" took form in her mind. That evening in her hotel room she composed the poem in full. It lay forgotten in her notebook until she discovered it two years later and sent it to the *Congregationalist* magazine. It was published, appropriately, on July 4, 1895. In 1904 she revised the text and it was printed in the Boston *Evening Transcript*. In 1912, after another revision of the text, Bates's poem was joined with a tune written in 1882 by Samuel Ward (1847–1903), a New Jersey organist and music store owner.

Bates, the descendant of early New England settlers and the daughter of a Congregational minister, was a lifelong teacher and author. She eventually became head of the English department at Wellesley, wrote twenty books and volumes of poetry, and received several honorary degrees. She would never take any money for her poem, for she believed it was her gift to her country.

This song is more than a look at our natural resources, beautiful as they are. It is an affirmation of our early pioneers who took freedom with them as they traveled west. And finally it is a prayer for God's help and guidance that America in the future can truly be a great land. Kenneth Osbeck, in *101 More Hymn Stories,* quotes Bates as saying, "We must match the greatness of our country with the goodness of personal godly living."

"America the Beautiful" became popular during World War I, and reportedly it was sung by a group of American soldiers in Verdun, France, on the day the war ended. Forty-two years later, in the summer of 1960, this hymn was played from the communications satellite Echo I, orbiting a thousand miles above the earth.

Now one hundred years old, "America the Beautiful" has traveled great distances, figuratively and literally, to become our most-loved national song.

O beautiful for spacious skies,
For amber waves of grain,
For purple mountain majesties
Above the fruited plain!
America! America!
God shed His grace on thee,
And crown thy good with brotherhood
From sea to shining sea!

O beautiful for pilgrim feet,
Whose stern, impassioned stress
A thoroughfare for freedom beat
Across the wilderness!
America! America!
God mend thine ev'ry flaw,
Confirm thy soul in self-control,
Thy liberty in law!

O beautiful for heroes proved
In liberating strife,
Who more than self their country loved,
And mercy more than life!
America! America!
May God thy gold refine
Till all success be nobleness
And ev'ry gain divine!

O beautiful for patriot dream
That sees beyond the years
Thine alabaster cities gleam
Undimmed by human tears!
America! America!
God shed His grace on thee,
And crown thy good with brotherhood
From sea to shining sea!

George Bennard (1873–1958)

The Old Rugged Cross

The most popular hymn of the midtwentieth century, "The Old Rugged Cross" is considered a modern gospel song. Written in 1913, it became instantly popular in part because it was used immediately by Homer Rodeheaver, song leader for Billy Sunday's evangelistic crusades. A radio station in Columbus, Ohio, once had a contest to discover people's favorite songs, religious and secular. "The Old Rugged Cross" not only took first place but scored more votes than all the other songs combined. The radio program "Sunday Evening Gatherings," hosted by Seth and "Ma" Parker, asked listeners to name their favorite hymns. "The Old Rugged Cross" topped the list by six thousand votes! I remember, in my youth, attending evangelistic services conducted by my own father when this hymn was often sung.

George Bennard, the hymn's author, was the son of a coal miner and himself worked in the mines from the age of fifteen to support his widowed mother. Converted at a Salvation Army meeting, he and his wife later became officers in the Salvation Army. Eventually he went into the Methodist ministry and spent most of his time conducting evangelistic services in Michigan and New York.

The inspiration for "The Old Rugged Cross" came out of a difficult period in Bennard's life. He composed the tune first, and then, as he said, "The words of the finished hymn were put into my heart in answer to my own need." A historical marker in front of the Delta Tau Delta fraternity house at Albion College in Albion, Michigan, indicates where he was staying when he began writing the hymn. It was first sung in a church in Pokagon, Michigan, and later introduced to the general public at the Chicago Evangelistic Institute. The Reverend Bennard's ministry continued for forty more years, during which time he wrote additional hymns, but none received the acclaim and popularity of "The Old Rugged Cross."

On a hill far away stood an old rugged Cross,
    The emblem of suff'ring and shame;
And I love that old cross, where the dearest and best
    For a world of lost sinners was slain.

Refrain
So I'll cherish the old rugged Cross,
    Till my trophies at last I lay down.
I will cling to the old rugged Cross,
    And exchange it someday for a crown.

Oh, that old rugged Cross, so despised by the world,
    Has a wondrous attraction for me;
For the dear Lamb of God left His glory above
    To bear it to dark Calvary.

In the old rugged Cross, stained with Blood so divine,
    A wondrous beauty I see;
For 'twas on that old Cross Jesus suffered and died
    To pardon and sanctify me.

To the old rugged Cross I will ever be true,
    Its shame and reproach gladly bear.
Then He'll call me someday to my home far away,
    Where His glory forever I'll share.

Sanford F. Bennett (1836–1898)

Sweet By and By

Another popular gospel hymn, "Sweet By and By," was written in thirty minutes on the counter of a drugstore in Elkhorn, Wisconsin. Its author, Sanford Bennett, had been editor of the Elkhorn newspaper prior to enlisting in the army during the Civil War. When he returned to Elkhorn after the war he decided to leave the newspaper business and open a drugstore.

Bennett had a good friend named Joseph Webster, an excellent violinist with whom he sometimes collaborated in song writing. Webster suffered from severe mood swings that caused him to have periods of depression. To raise his spirits, Bennett would give him new songs on which to work.

One day Webster came into the drugstore in a low mood. He poured out his troubles to Bennett but then finally said, "Everything will be all right in the by and by." Going behind the counter, Bennett took out a pad, wrote feverishly for a few minutes, and handed the sheet to Webster. "Here's your prescription. I believe it will do wonders in changing your mood." The prescription was the text to this hymn.

Webster took out his violin, started working on a tune, and soon had written the music we know today. Two customers who had entered the drugstore in the previous minutes joined them in singing it. Passersby on the street, hearing the music in the drugstore, came in and added their voices to the singing. That song, whose words and music were written in thirty minutes, would eventually become the universally loved hymn "Sweet By and By."

There's a land that is fairer than day,
And by faith we can see it afar;
For the Father waits over the way,
To prepare us a dwelling place there.

Chorus
In the sweet by and by,
We shall meet on that beautiful shore,
In the sweet by and by,
We shall meet on that beautiful shore.

We shall sing on that beautiful shore
The melodious songs of the blest,
And our spirits shall sorrow no more,
Not a sigh for the blessing of rest.

To our bountiful Father above,
We will offer our tribute of praise,
For the glorious gift of His love,
And the blessings that hallow our days.

Phillips Brooks (1835–1893)

O Little Town of Bethlehem

A visit to the Holy Land inspired the beloved Christmas carol "O Little Town of Bethlehem." On Christmas Eve in 1865, Phillips Brooks traveled from Jerusalem to Bethlehem, stopping on the way to stand on the hills overlooking the little town where the shepherds had been tending their flocks on the night of Jesus' birth. Like Brooks, I too have visited Bethlehem on Christmas Eve. It was a profound spiritual experience to look out over Shepherd's Fields and sit in an outdoor courtyard near the area where Jesus was born, singing this hymn and listening to the familiar words from the Bible describing his birth.

Three years after his visit, Brooks was planning a Christmas program for the children of his church in Philadelphia, and he searched for a suitable hymn for them to use. He remembered his experience in Bethlehem and wrote a poem about it. He gave it to his organist and church-school superintendent, Lewis Redner (1831–1908), asking him to write a simple tune. Redner struggled with the assignment. By the Saturday night before the service he still had not composed a tune. In the middle of the night he awoke with the melody in his mind, and he finished the harmonies early the next morning just in time for the Christmas program. Redner always felt the tune was a gift from God.

Phillips Brooks was one of America's greatest preachers. Born in Boston, educated at Harvard and at Episcopal Theological Seminary in Virginia, he was a brilliant and cultured man. He was six feet, six inches tall, with a commanding and elegant physical presence. He also was loving and warmhearted, and all people, especially children, were drawn to him. Known as the "Prince of the Pulpit," he was a forceful evangelical preacher and was credited with slowing the spread of Unitarianism, which had taken root in New England's congregational churches. In addition to serving Holy Trinity Church in Philadelphia, he was rector of Trinity Church in Boston for twenty-two years. His sermons are considered classics of American literature; the first volume, published in 1878, sold over two hundred thousand copies.

Brooks loved hymns. He memorized hundreds of them in his childhood and would sing one or two every morning while getting dressed. Brooks died suddenly at the age of fifty-eight, shortly after he had been appointed bishop of Massachusetts. "O Little Town of Bethlehem" is the only one of his hymns to remain popular.

O little town of Bethlehem,
How still we see thee lie!
Above thy deep and dreamless sleep
The silent stars go by.
Yet in thy dark streets shineth
The everlasting Light;
The hopes and fears of all the years
Are met in thee tonight.

For Christ is born of Mary;
And gathered all above,
While mortals sleep, the angels keep
Their watch of wond'ring love.
O morning stars, together
Proclaim the holy birth;
And praises sing to God, the King,
And peace to men on earth.

How silently, how silently
The wondrous Gift is giv'n!
So God imparts to human hearts

The blessings of His heav'n.
No ear may hear His coming;
But in this world of sin,
Where meek souls will receive Him still,
The dear Christ enters in.

O holy Child of Bethlehem,
Descend on us, we pray.
Cast out our sin, and enter in;
Be born in us today.
We hear the Christmas angels
The great glad tidings tell.
O, come to us, abide with us,
Our Lord, Emmanuel.

Edward C. Caswall (1814–1878)

During the midnineteenth century, some leaders in the Anglican Church reacted to the evangelical emphasis on personal conversion and nontraditional methods of worship used by the Wesley brothers and others who followed them. These Anglican leaders sought to bring about spiritual renewal within the Anglican Church by increasing ritual and liturgy and trying to restore the church to the way it had been in previous centuries. This renewal effort was called the Oxford Movement because it began with a sermon delivered at Oxford University by a parish priest named John Keble.

As part of the Oxford Movement, many hymns were translated from ancient sources into English in an attempt to rejuvenate the church. Edward Caswall, an Anglican priest and a leader in the Oxford Movement, translated about two hundred hymn texts. He, like several others, eventually became a Roman Catholic and continued to translate hymns for use in that church. Two of the best-known hymns he translated are "When Morning Gilds the Skies" and "Jesus, the Very Thought of Thee."

When Morning Gilds the Skies

The text of "When Morning Gilds the Skies" was written by an unknown German author as a hymn of praise. We should praise God in the morning, in the evening, at work, and at prayer, in good times and in bad, "thro' all the ages long." Originally there were twenty-eight stanzas, but only four are generally used today.

The tune was composed in 1868 by Joseph Barnby (1838–1896), a leading composer and music director in England who was knighted by Queen Victoria in 1892.

When morning gilds the skies,
My heart awaking cries,
May Jesus Christ be praised!
Alike at work and pray'r,
To Jesus I repair.
May Jesus Christ be praised!

The night becomes as day
When from the heart we say,
May Jesus Christ be praised!
The pow'rs of darkness fear,
When this sweet chant they hear,
May Jesus Christ be praised!

In heav'n's eternal bliss
The loveliest strain is this,
May Jesus Christ be praised!
Let earth, and sea, and sky,
From depth to height reply,
May Jesus Christ be praised!

Be this, while life is mine,
My canticle divine,
May Jesus Christ be praised!

Be this th'eternal song
Thro' all the ages long,
May Jesus Christ be praised!

Jesus, the Very Thought of Thee

One of the earliest hymns still in use today, "Jesus, the Very Thought of Thee" is attributed to Bernard of Clairvaux, a twelfth-century mystic (1091–1153). In a time of moral decadence of both civil and religious leaders, Bernard stood out as a monk of personal integrity, spiritual depth, and considerable influence.

From its earliest beginnings this hymn has had a place among the great devotional texts of the Christian faith. John Dykes (1823–1876), who also composed the music for "Holy, Holy, Holy," set Bernard of Clairvaux's text to music and named the tune "St. Agnes," after a thirteen-year-old girl who was killed in A.D. 304 because she would not renounce her Christian faith. Caswall translated the hymn in 1849.

Jesus, the very thought of Thee
With sweetness fills my breast;
But sweeter far Thy face to see,
And in Thy presence rest.

25

No voice can sing, no heart can frame,
Nor can the mem'ry find
A sweeter sound than Thy blest name,
O Saviour of mankind!

O Hope of ev'ry contrite heart,
O Joy of all the meek,
To those who fall, how kind Thou art!
How good to those who seek!

But what to those who find? Ah, this
Nor tongue nor pen can show.
The love of Jesus, what it is
None but His loved ones know.

George Croly (1780–1860)

Spirit of God, Descend upon My Heart

In 1854 George Croly, an Anglican minister, decided that his congregation needed a new collection of hymns, so he compiled one himself. In that collection he included a hymn of his own, "Spirit of God, Descend upon My Heart." He printed one edition of the hymnbook and then used the copies in his church's worship service. One day a fire engulfed his church, destroying most of the new hymnals. Fortunately for us not all were lost, for this hymn, the only one written by Croly that is still sung today, beautifully expresses the need for the Holy Spirit to fill our lives.

George Croly was born in Ireland, attended Trinity College in Dublin, and was ordained in the Church of England. Shortly after his thirtieth birthday he moved to London to continue his writing career, which included poetry, fiction, and biography. He was asked by his bishop to reopen a church, located in one of the most depressed areas of London, that had been vacant for more than one hundred years. Because of his zealous preaching and engaging personality, he soon attracted large crowds, and the church began to grow.

The tune used today for "Spirit of God, Descend upon My Heart" was written in 1870 by an English church organist, Frederick Atkinson (1841–1897). Originally intended for the hymn "Abide with Me," it became a perfect complement to the poetic phrases and quiet spirit of Croly's text.

Spirit of God, descend upon my heart.
Wean it from earth; through all its pulses move.
Stoop to my weakness, mighty as Thou art,
And make me love Thee as I ought to love.

Hast Thou not bid us love Thee, God and King?
All, all Thine own: soul, heart, and strength and mind!
I see Thy cross—there teach my heart to cling.
O let me seek Thee, and O let me find!

Teach me to feel that Thou art always nigh;
Teach me the struggles of the soul to bear,
To check the rising doubt, the rebel sigh;
Teach me the patience of unanswered prayer.

Teach me to love Thee as Thine angels love,
One holy passion filling all my frame:
The baptism of the heav'n-descended Dove;
My heart an altar, and Thy love the flame.

Fanny Crosby (1820–1915)

Fanny Crosby has been called America's best-loved gospel song writer. She wrote more than eight thousand songs during her remarkable life that spanned ninety-five years. Tragically blinded at six weeks of age by a quack doctor who had incorrectly treated an eye infection, Fanny Crosby used her affliction throughout her life to stress the profound care and guidance God gives to us.

Crosby had no formal education before the age of fifteen, when she entered the New York School for the Blind. She was bright and a quick learner; for eleven years after her graduation she taught language and history at the school.

She also wrote poetry and music and earned three thousand dollars in royalties for one of her secular songs, "Rosalie the Prairie Flower." At the age of forty-one she was challenged by a well-known church musician, W. B. Bradbury, to try writing hymns. With that suggestion, Fanny Crosby found her mission in life.

Crosby composed all her poems in her head, dictating them to friends. She had a remarkable memory, often reciting verbatim entire books of the Bible.

Her later years were spent traveling, singing, and lecturing, and it is said she died with a smile on her face at the age of ninety-five.

Two of my favorite Crosby hymns are "All the Way My Saviour Leads Me" and "Blessed Assurance."

All the Way My Saviour Leads Me

An answer to prayer resulted in the hymn "All the Way My Saviour Leads Me." All her life Crosby chose to live among the poor in some of the worst slums in New York City, believing she could minister more effectively to them by living among them. She and her husband, Alexander Van Alstyne, a blind musician whom she had met at the New York School for the Blind, gave away everything beyond their basic needs.

One day in the fall of 1874, Crosby realized she didn't have enough money to pay the rent, so she began to pray about it, as she did about every problem in her life. Shortly thereafter her doorbell rang. When she answered it, the stranger standing there put something in her hand. It was the exact amount she needed for the rent. Later that day she wrote this hymn. She believed God had sent this money to her, and she responded with gratitude, believing that if we trust God in everything he will lead us in amazing ways. The poem was later put to music by Robert Lowry (1826–1899), a Baptist minister.

Although she lived in poverty, Fanny Crosby had many wealthy friends and met prominent people through them, including Presidents Grover Cleveland and Ulysses S. Grant. Because of those contacts, she was asked to read one of her poems in the U.S. Senate, the first time a woman had spoken publicly in the Senate chamber.

All the way my Saviour leads me.
What have I to ask beside?
Can I doubt His tender mercy

Who thro' life has been my Guide?
Heav'nly peace, divinest comfort,
　　Here by faith in Him to dwell!
For I know, whate'er befall me,
　　Jesus doeth all things well.

All the way my Saviour leads me,
　　Cheers each winding path I tread,
Gives me grace for ev'ry trial,
　　Feeds me with the living bread.
Tho' my weary steps may falter,
　　And my soul athirst may be,
Gushing from the Rock before me,
　　Lo! a spring of joy I see.

All the way my Saviour leads me.
　　Oh, the fullness of His love!
Perfect rest to me is promised
　　In my Father's house above.
When my spirit, clothed, immortal
　　Wings its flight to realms of day.
This my song thro' endless ages—
　　Jesus led me all the way.

Blessed Assurance

"Blessed Assurance" may be Fanny Crosby's most enduring legacy. The tune was composed first by her good friend Phoebe Knapp (1839–1908), who had married the founder of the Metropolitan Life Insurance Company. As Kenneth Osbeck reported in *101 Hymn Stories,* Phoebe Knapp played the music for Fanny and asked, "What does this tune say?"

Fanny replied immediately, "Why that says, 'Blessed assurance, Jesus is mine.'"

Many of Crosby's hymns, such as "Blessed Assurance," emphasize conversion, hope, and new life through Christ. She herself had been converted at a revival at North Broadway Tabernacle in New York City in 1850, and she spent the rest of her life trying to spread the gospel, especially to the down-and-outers of the Bowery mission. Many of her hymns were written for use at the mission.

Blessed assurance, Jesus is mine!
Oh, what a foretaste of glory divine!
Heir of salvation, purchase of God,
Born of His Spirit, washed in His blood!

Refrain
This is my story, this is my song,
Praising my Saviour all the day long.
This is my story, this is my song.
Praising my Saviour all the day long.

Perfect submission, perfect delight!
Visions of rapture now burst on my sight!
Angels descending bring from above
Echoes of mercy, whispers of love.

Perfect submission, all is at rest.
I in my Saviour am happy and blest;
Watching and waiting, looking above,
Filled with His goodness, lost in His love.

Timothy Dwight (1752–1817)

I Love Thy Kingdom, Lord

Timothy Dwight is known as America's great pioneer in hymn writing. He also was one of the most gifted and influential men in the early history of the United States. Born in 1752 to the daughter of preacher and evangelist Jonathan Edwards, Dwight graduated with highest honors from Yale University at the age of seventeen. During his adult life he served as chaplain with George Washington during the Revolutionary War, became a Congregational minister, a successful farmer, a representative to the Connecticut state legislature, a faculty member at Yale, and then president of that institution from 1795 to 1815.

Dwight had an insatiable desire to learn, and he mastered any subject he undertook, starting with the Bible at age four and Latin at age seven. His gifts of preaching, teaching, and writing were immense. At Yale he taught literature, oratory, ethics, metaphysics, logic, and theology. Under his preaching the entire moral and religious climate of the university changed. He ignited a spiritual awakening on campus that spread to several other colleges in New England.

In addition to hymns, his writings included literary, scholarly, and theological works. "I Love Thy Kingdom, Lord" was written in 1801 while Dwight was president of Yale. This is the oldest American hymn still sung today. It was one of several he wrote for a revision of Isaac Watts's *Psalms and Hymns,* in which, following the American Revolution, references to Great Britain were removed. The tune, thought to be an adaptation of a work by George Frederick Handel, first appeared in a collection of songs by Aaron Williams (1731–1776), music director of Scottish Presbyterian Church in London.

All the considerable accomplishments of Timothy Dwight were achieved in spite of serious physical problems. A case of smallpox had caused a deteriorating eye condition that produced not only constant intense pain but also an inability to read for more than fifteen minutes at a time each day. This condition lasted for forty years, beginning when he was twenty-five years of age. Timothy Dwight's faith and reliance on God were evidenced throughout his remarkable life.

I love Thy kingdom, Lord,
The house of Thine abode,
The Church our blest Redeemer saved
With His own precious blood.

I love Thy Church, O God!
Her walls before Thee stand,
Dear as the apple of Thine eye,
And graven on Thy hand.

For her my tears shall fall;
For her my pray'rs ascend;

To her my cares and toils be giv'n
Till toils and cares shall end.

Beyond my highest joy
I prize her heav'nly ways,
Her sweet communion, solemn vows,
Her hymns of love and praise.

Jesus, Thou friend divine,
Our Savior and our King,
Thy hand from every snare and foe
Shall great deliverance bring.

Sure as Thy truth shall last,
To Zion shall be giv'n
The brightest glories earth can yield,
And brighter bliss of heav'n.

Charlotte Elliott (1789–1871)

Just as I Am

As a bedridden invalid for fifty of her eighty-two years, Charlotte Elliott gave the world one of its most beloved and well-known hymns. Prior to the age of thirty, Charlotte was a vivacious and energetic young woman, excelling as a portrait painter and poet. As her health began to fail and she had to give up her painting, she experienced bouts of depression and frustration. During one of these times a Swiss evangelist, Cesar Malan, visited her bedside. Discussing with her the love of God, he is purported to have said, "Just come to him as you are, Charlotte." She then experienced a spiritual awakening that was the turning point of her life.

Twelve years later, in 1834, again frustrated because she could not do something useful to help raise money for a special project in her brother's church, she remembered Dr. Malan's admonition to "come as you are." During a sleepless night she wrote the words to this hymn, and they were later set to music by William Bradbury (1816–1868), a well-known organist and choirmaster. As it turned out, this hymn brought in more money for the church project than all other money raisers combined.

Charlotte's brother, a clergyman, said that with this one hymn his sister had influenced more people than he would in his lifetime of ministry. Charlotte's legacy is the message that everyone can be used by God regardless of his or her circumstances.

Just as I am, without one plea
But that Thy blood was shed for me,
And that Thou bidd'st me come to Thee,
O Lamb of God, I come! I come!

Just as I am, and waiting not
To rid my soul of one dark blot,
To Thee whose blood can cleanse each spot,
O Lamb of God, I come! I come!

Just as I am, tho' tossed about
With many a conflict, many a doubt,
Fightings and fears within, without,
O Lamb of God, I come! I come!

Just as I am—poor, wretched, blind;
Sight, riches, healing of the mind,
Yea, all I need in Thee to find,
O Lamb of God, I come! I come!

Just as I am—Thou wilt receive,
Wilt welcome, pardon, cleanse, relieve;
Because Thy promise I believe,
O Lamb of God, I come! I come!

Frederick W. Faber (1814–1863)

Frederick W. Faber was an Anglican priest greatly influenced by the Oxford Movement in nineteenth-century England. Raised as a strict Calvinist by his minister father, Faber grew up with strong anti–Roman Catholic sentiments. He even published articles outlining the "error" of Catholic teachings. At the same time he worked for upgrading the liturgical and ceremonial aspects of Anglican worship to offset the influences of the Wesleyan movement, which he and other Oxford Movement members thought were undermining the church. Finally, in 1845 at the age of thirty-one, he decided to leave the Anglican Church and become a Roman Catholic. He was ordained a priest in 1846, took the name of Wilfred, and founded a religious community in Birmingham, England.

Faber realized the impact of hymn singing in the Protestant church and wanted to firmly establish that practice in the Catholic church. All one hundred fifty of his hymns were written after he became a Catholic. Two of his finest are "Faith of Our Fathers" and "There's a Wideness in God's Mercy."

Faith of Our Fathers

The one hymn that has meant the most to me since young boyhood is "Faith of Our Fathers." I can still hear its stirring words ringing out in the small churches my father pastored while I was growing up. It is a hymn I have requested to be sung on every special occasion in my church life.

Written in 1849 to commemorate the church's martyrs who died for their faith, this hymn reminds me that there is always a sturdy body of committed men and women who stand by Jesus without regard to popularity or cost. This hymn teaches that no matter what may come, the Christian faith is an alive, viable, vital way of life, a practical gospel that works when worked.

The tune was composed in 1864 by Henry F. Hemy (1818–1888), and the final eight measures and the refrain were added in 1884 by James Walton (1821–1905).

Faith of our fathers, living still
In spite of dungeon, fire, and sword!

Oh, how our hearts beat high with joy
Whene'er we hear that glorious word!
Faith of our fathers! holy faith!
We will be true to thee till death!

Our fathers, chained in prisons dark,
Were still in heart and conscience free.
How sweet would be their children's fate
If they, like them, could die for thee!
Faith of our fathers! holy faith!
We will be true to thee till death!

Faith of our fathers! we will love
Both friend and foe in all our strife;
And preach thee, too, as love knows how,
By kindly words and virtuous life.
Faith of our fathers! holy faith!
We will be true to thee till death!

There's a Wideness in God's Mercy

"There's a Wideness in God's Mercy" was part of a thirteen-verse poem entitled "Souls of Men, Why Will Ye Scatter?" first published in 1854. Faber compares the scope of God's mercy to the sea that is so vast we cannot comprehend it. The tune was composed by a teenage girl for her high school graduation ceremonies. Lizzie Tourjee (1858–1913) came from a musical family. Her father was founder of the New England Conservatory of Music and a respected musician and music publisher. He joined Faber's hymn and his daughter's tune together in a hymnal published in 1878.

There's a wideness in God's mercy
Like the wideness of the sea;
There's a kindness in His justice
Which is more than liberty.

There is welcome for the sinner,
And more graces for the good.
There is mercy with the Saviour;
There is healing in His blood.

For the love of God is broader
Than the measure of man's mind;
And the heart of the Eternal
Is most wonderfully kind.

If our love were but more simple,
We should take Him at His word;
And our lives would be all sunshine
In the sweetness of our Lord.

John Fawcett (1740–1817)

Blest Be the Tie That Binds

"Blest Be the Tie That Binds" commemorates a very touching moment in the life of its author. Born in Yorkshire, England, to a family of limited means, John Fawcett was sent to London at the age of thirteen to be apprenticed to a tailor because his parents wanted him to learn a trade. This was the era of the Wesleyan revival, and young Fawcett, now sixteen, was greatly influenced by the preaching of famed evangelist George Whitefield. His conversion changed the direction of his life, and ten years later, after finishing his apprenticeship, he was ordained into the Baptist ministry.

Fawcett's first church was a small parish in Wainsgate, England. He was a wonderful pastor, serving the people with energy and devotion, and they loved him and his growing family in return. However, it was a struggle to make ends meet. So when he received a call some years later to the prestigious Carter's Lane Baptist Church in London, he felt he should accept.

The story is told that on the day of his departure his beloved parishioners surrounded his wagon to bid him farewell. There was such sadness on their faces and in their words of good-bye that Mrs. Fawcett said to her husband, "John, I cannot bear to leave." Evidently he was having similar thoughts, for he immediately had the wagon unloaded and their possessions put back in the parsonage. A few days later he wrote "Blest Be the Tie That Binds" as an expression of his love for his people. That tie bound them together until his death in 1817.

John Fawcett's influence and fame spread far beyond rural England, however. In 1777 he founded a school for young ministers. He also became an outstanding writer and scholar. One particular essay on anger, written in 1780, so impressed King George III that the monarch promised to grant any favor Fawcett might request. Needing nothing for himself, Fawcett requested a pardon for the son of a friend who had been sentenced to death for forgery. The request was granted. In 1811, in recognition of his many accomplishments, America's Brown University conferred on him the degree of Doctor of Divinity. It was quite an honor for a poor preacher who had spent his life ministering in a small, rural parish in northern England.

"Blest Be the Tie That Binds" is often sung at farewell gatherings. It helps people remember the good times and the faith that binds them together. At my father's memorial service in Lynchburg, Ohio, seven ministers who had known and loved him, including my brother Leonard and myself, gathered in the front of the church, joined hands, and sang "Blest Be the Tie That Binds." It was our last farewell to a great man and a great Christian.

The tune was written by Hans G. Nageli (1773–1836).

Blest be the tie that binds
Our hearts in Christian love;
The fellowship of kindred minds
Is like to that above.

Before our Father's throne
We pour our ardent prayers;
Our fears, our hopes, our aims are one,
Our comforts and our cares.

We share our mutual woes,
Our mutual burdens bear;
And often for each other flows
The sympathizing tear.

When we asunder part
It gives us inward pain;
But we shall still be joined in heart,
And hope to meet again.

Harry Emerson Fosdick (1878–1969)

God of Grace

The great Riverside Church in New York City opened in October of 1930. On the banks of the Hudson River, this magnificent building had been made possible by the generosity of John D. Rockefeller, Jr., a member of the church. The previous summer, while vacationing in Maine, Dr. Harry Emerson Fosdick, Riverside's minister, wrote a hymn especially for the opening of that building. On October 5, 1930, and again at the church's dedication, February 9, 1931, the magnificent sanctuary echoed with this new hymn, written by their minister to the glory of God.

Fosdick had a long and distinguished career in New York City. For twenty years he pastored Riverside Church (known as the Park Avenue Baptist Church before it moved to its present location). He taught homiletics and practical theology at Union Theological Seminary for thirty-five years, wrote thirty-two books, and pioneered in radio ministry in this country. I was privileged to know him personally and considered him one of the most forceful and dynamic preachers I've ever heard.

For his hymn Fosdick had chosen the tune "Regent Square," which is used today with "Angels from the Realms of Glory." In 1935 the current tune was joined to the text, much to Fosdick's displeasure. However, it proved to be a good move, for since that time "God of Grace" has gained a place among the church's great hymns.

God of grace and God of glory,
On Thy people pour Thy power;
Crown Thine ancient Church's story,
Bring her bud to glorious flower.
Grant us wisdom, Grant us courage,
For the facing of this hour,
For the facing of this hour.

Lo! the hosts of evil round us
Scorn Thy Christ, assail His ways!
From the fears that long have bound us,
Free our hearts to faith and praise.
Grant us wisdom, Grant us courage,
For the living of these days,
For the living of these days.

Cure Thy children's warring madness;
Bend our pride to Thy control;
Shame our wanton, selfish gladness,
Rich in things and poor in soul.
Grant us wisdom, Grant us courage,
Lest we miss Thy kingdom's goal,
Lest we miss Thy kingdom's goal.

Set our feet on lofty places,
Gird our lives that they may be
Armored with all Christlike graces
In the fight to set men free.
Grant us wisdom, Grant us courage,
That we fail not man nor Thee,
That we fail not man nor Thee.

Joseph H. Gilmore (1834–1918)

He Leadeth Me

On March 26, 1862, Joseph Gilmore, a twenty-eight-year-old Baptist minister, was preaching at the Wednesday evening prayer service of the First Baptist Church in Philadelphia. He spoke on the Twenty-third Psalm. Later that night, over refreshments at the home of Deacon Thomas S. Wattson, he discussed with Wattson the sermon and the events of the Civil War then in progress. Kenneth W. Osbeck's *101 Hymn Stories* gives Gilmore's account of how his hymn came into being: "During our conversation, the blessedness of God's leading so grew upon me that I took out my pencil, wrote the hymn just as it stands today, handed it to my wife, and thought no more of it. She sent it, without my knowledge, to the *Watchman and Reflector* magazine and there it first appeared in print."

William Bradbury (1816–1868), a well-known musician and composer, first saw the text of "He Leadeth Me" in the *Watchman and Reflector* in 1863. He wrote the tune for it, adding two additional lines to the chorus.

In 1865 Gilmore traveled to Rochester, New York, to preach in the Second Baptist Church. His account of that evening follows:

"Upon entering the chapel, I took up a hymnbook, thinking, 'I wonder what they sing.' The book opened up at 'He Leadeth Me,' and that was the first time I knew that my hymn had found a place among the songs of the church."

When the First Baptist Church in Philadelphia was torn down in 1926 to make way for an office building, a bronze plaque was put in the corner of the new building inscribed with the first verse of "He Leadeth Me." "This was done," the inscription reads, "in recognition of the beauty and fame of this beloved hymn, and in remembrance of its distinguished author."

In addition to pastoring several churches, Joseph Gilmore was also a college professor. While he published many books and wrote other hymns, he will always be known for this particular one, written in a moment of inspiration and preserved for us by Mrs. Gilmore.

He leadeth me! Oh, blessed tho't!
Oh, words with heav'nly comfort fraught!
Whate'er I do, where'er I be,
Still 'tis God's hand that leadeth me.

Refrain
He leadeth me, He leadeth me,
By His own hand He leadeth me.
His faithful follower I would be,
For by His hand He leadeth me.

Sometimes 'mid scenes of deepest gloom,
Sometimes where Eden's bowers bloom,
By waters still, o'er troubled sea,
Still 'tis His hand that leadeth me!

Lord, I would clasp Thy hand in mine,
Nor ever murmur nor repine,
Content, whatever lost I see,
Since 'tis my God that leadeth me!

And when my task on earth is done,
When, by Thy grace, the vict'ry's won,
E'en death's cold wave I will not flee,
Since God thro' Jordan leadeth me.

Washington Gladden (1836–1918)

O Master, Let Me Walk with Thee

"O Master, Let Me Walk with Thee" was written as a devotional reading and published in *Sunday Afternoon,* a periodical edited by Washington Gladden. But when someone suggested the poem would make a good hymn text, Gladden chose a tune by H. Percy Smith (1825–1898) that had originally been composed for a different hymn. "O Master Let Me Walk with Thee" as we know it today was published in 1880.

The spirit of the hymn is in marked contrast to the life and ministry of its author. Gladden was militant, forceful, and fearless

51

in his belief that the gospel should affect the social, political, and economic life of America. Following the Civil War, the country was caught up in the industrial revolution, which led to exploitation, excesses, and corruption. Gladden, as a minister, felt it was his duty to address those issues.

When he was religion editor of the *New York Independent*, Gladden exposed the graft of the Tweed Ring, a group of politicians who controlled the New York City treasury. While serving the First Congregational Church of Columbus, Ohio, he attacked John D. Rockefeller for his gift of one hundred thousand dollars to the Congregational Board of Foreign Missions. Gladden called the money tainted because of Rockefeller's connection with Standard Oil, a company Gladden accused of monopolistic practices. Gladden also served as a labor negotiator in 1883 in the telegraphers' strike and in the Hocking Valley coal strike of 1884. Gladden was criticized, both by the secular press for his ideas and by the religious press and many ministers for involving himself in what they called nonspiritual matters. Gladden firmly believed that the church should exert an influence in the life of the community, and he continued to speak out on the issues as he saw them. Today, however, he is known for the devotional hymn published as a poem and meant for quiet meditation and reflection.

O Master, let me walk with Thee
In lowly paths of service free.
Tell me Thy secret; help me bear
The strain of toil, the fret of care.

Help me the slow of heart to move
By some clear, winning word of love.
Teach me the wayward feet to stay,
And guide them in the homeward way.

Teach me Thy patience! still with Thee
In closer, dearer company,
In work that keeps faith sweet and strong,
In trust that triumphs over wrong.

In hope that sends a shining ray
Far down the future's broadening way,
In peace that only Thou canst give,
With Thee, O Master, let me live.

Frances R. Havergal (1836–1879)

Take My Life

Frances Havergal had one goal in life, and that was to be a true servant of Jesus Christ. At the age of four she started to memorize the Bible, and by age seven she was writing poetry. God blessed her with a musical talent that would have brought her riches and fame in the secular world, but she chose to use her gifts in service to God. Although in poor health most of her life, she was an avid student of the Bible, learning Greek and Hebrew to help her in her studies.

"Take My Life" was written in 1874. Havergal was spending the week with ten friends, whom she prayed for one by one during those days. Lindajo McKim, in the *Presbyterian Hymnal Companion,* quotes Havergal's account of that visit and how the hymn came into being: "There were ten persons in the house, some unconverted and long prayed-for, some converted but not rejoicing Christians. God gave me the prayer, 'Lord, give me all in this house!' And He just *did.* Before I left the house, everyone had got a blessing! The last night of my visit . . . I was too happy to sleep, and passed most of the night in renewal of my own consecration, and these little couplets formed themselves and chimed in my heart one after another, till they finished with 'Ever, only, *all* for Thee.'"

The tune for "Take My Life" was composed by a Swiss evangelist, Henri A. Cesar Malan (1787–1864), who wrote more than one thousand hymn tunes. It was put with Havergal's text and published in 1878. Later Havergal wrote a book based on this hymn, entitled *Kept for the Master's Work*. After Havergal's death her sister collected all her work in one volume and published it.

Also in 1878 the words of the third verse of her hymn were made real in Frances's own life. She felt God was asking her to give away her "silver and gold," so she packed up fifty pieces of jewelry and ornaments, plus a jewel cabinet, and sent them to the church missionary house for distribution.

Havergal had a lifelong correspondence with the American hymn writer Fanny Crosby. Though the two never met, they were much alike in their dedication to the poor and needy, their spiritual fervor, and their literary achievements.

Take my life, and let it be
Consecrated, Lord, to Thee.
Take my hands, and let them move
At the impulse of Thy love,
At the impulse of Thy love.

Take my feet, and let them be
Swift and beautiful for Thee.
Take my voice, and let me sing
Always, only, for my King;
Always, only, for my King.

Take my lips, and let them be
Filled with messages for Thee.
Take my silver and my gold;
Not a mite would I withhold,
Not a mite would I withhold.

Take my will and make it Thine;
It shall be no longer mine.
Take my heart; it is Thine own!
It shall be Thy royal throne.
It shall be Thy royal throne.

Take my love; my God, I pour
At Thy feet its treasure store.
Take myself and I will be
Ever, only, all for Thee;
Ever, only, all for Thee.

Annie S. Hawks (1835–1918)

I Need Thee Every Hour

One day in 1872, as Annie Hawks was going about the ordinary tasks of keeping a household and raising three children, she wondered how anyone could get through a day without experiencing the nearness of God. Already a published poet of some stature, she was used to translating her thoughts into verse, so she jotted down the text of "I Need Thee Every Hour" that very day. Later she showed it to the minister of her church in Brooklyn, Robert Lowry (1826–1899), who had encouraged her in her writing. Lowry, himself an accomplished musician, immediately wrote the music and the chorus following each verse.

That same year, 1872, Dr. Lowry introduced this hymn at the national Baptist Sunday School Convention and later included it in a collection of Sunday school songs he published. Although he was a great orator and did not develop his musical talents until midlife, Robert Lowry is now known exclusively for his songs. His other hymn tunes of note are "Shall We Gather at the River" (written during an epidemic that claimed thousands of lives) and "All the Way My Saviour Leads Me," by Fanny Crosby.

"I Need Thee Every Hour" was popularized through the many crusades conducted by D. L. Moody and Ira Sankey in the United States and England. Sixteen years after writing this hymn, Annie Hawks found special comfort in its words as she grieved the loss of her husband.

Although she wrote more than four hundred hymn texts, this is the only one still sung today.

I need Thee ev'ry hour,
    Most gracious Lord;
No tender voice like Thine
    Can peace afford.

Refrain
I need Thee; oh, I need Thee!
    Ev'ry hour I need Thee!
Oh, bless me now, my Saviour;
    I come to Thee!

I need Thee ev'ry hour;
    Stay Thou nearby.
Temptations lose their pow'r
    When Thou art nigh.

I need Thee ev'ry hour,
    In joy or pain;
Come quickly and abide,
    Or life is vain.

I need Thee ev'ry hour,
    Most Holy One.
Oh, make me Thine indeed,·
    Thou blessed Son!

Reginald Heber (1783–1826)

Holy, Holy, Holy

Sir Alfred Lord Tennyson, poet laureate of England, regarded "Holy, Holy, Holy" as the world's greatest hymn. It was written by Reginald Heber to be sung in praise and adoration of God on Trinity Sunday. Through the years "Holy, Holy Holy" has brought majesty and reverence to worship services around the world, and it is one of my personal favorites.

Heber was born in Cheshire, England, to well-educated and well-to-do parents. After studying at Oxford, he was ordained an Anglican priest and served for sixteen years in an out-of-the-way village called Hodnet. Most of his hymns were written during these years for use in his parish. Heber believed that congregational singing greatly enhanced worship, and his book of hymns did much to popularize hymn singing throughout the Anglican Church.

In spite of serving a poor parish, far from the center of literary and religious activity, Heber became well known. He was a prolific writer, contributing poetry and essays to periodicals and journals. This literary talent was not unexpected, as he had won many awards for his poetry while a student at Oxford. In 1823, because of his interest in and support for foreign missions, he was sent to India as Bishop of Calcutta. His territory included Ceylon and Australia as well. The humid climate, travel, and stress of the responsibilities wore him down, and he died suddenly of a sunstroke at forty-three years of age. Even though a great life was cut short, Reginald Heber gave the world a lasting legacy with this one hymn.

The tune was composed by Dr. John Dykes (1823–1876), a leading church musician in England who wrote more than three hundred hymn tunes.

Holy, Holy, Holy, Lord God Almighty!
Early in the morning our song shall rise to Thee.
Holy, Holy, Holy! Merciful and Mighty!
God in three Persons, blessed Trinity!

Holy, Holy, Holy! All the saints adore Thee,
Casting down their golden crowns around the glassy sea;
Cherubim and seraphim falling down before Thee,
Which wert, and art, and evermore shalt be.

Holy, Holy, Holy! Tho' the darkness hide Thee,
Tho' the eye of sinful man Thy glory may not see,
Only Thou art holy; there is none beside Thee
Perfect in pow'r, in love, in purity.

Holy, Holy, Holy! Lord God Almighty!
All Thy works shall praise Thy name in earth, and sky, and
     sea.
Holy, Holy Holy! Merciful and Mighty!
God in three Persons, blessed Trinity!

Stuart K. Hine (1899–1989)

How Great Thou Art

The familiar hymn "How Great Thou Art" expresses God's majesty and power. It was first introduced in the United States in 1951 and made popular by Cliff Barrows and George Beverly Shea at Billy Graham crusades in the succeeding years. The original version was written in 1886 by the Reverend Carl Boberg (1859–1940), a Swedish preacher, editor, and statesman. Boberg was inspired to write the text when he visited a beautiful country home on the coast of Sweden and was caught in a rainstorm. Loud claps of thunder were followed by brilliant sun and the singing of birds, prompting Boberg to write a poem praising God for the beauty of creation. Some years later he was surprised to hear his poem being sung to an old Swedish melody.

The text was translated into several languages. In 1933 Stuart Hine, an English missionary in the Ukraine, learned the Russian translation and often sang it as a duet with his wife in the churches they served. Sometime later, on a trip through the mountains of Czechoslovakia, a thunderstorm broke out, and Hine, remembering this Russian song, composed original English words for the first three verses. He shared Boberg's awe for the power and majesty of God. Back home in England after World War II, Hine composed verse four and arranged the Swedish folk melody into the hymn we know today.

"How Great Thou Art" was printed in a gospel magazine in 1949 and then published in leaflet form. One of those leaflets came to the attention of George Beverly Shea in 1954, who sang it soon after at an evangelistic crusade. "How Great Thou Art" is now one of the hymns most universally loved by all Christians.

O Lord, my God! When I in awesome wonder
Consider all the worlds Thy hands have made,
I see the stars, I hear the rolling thunder,
Thy power throughout the universe displayed,

Refrain
Then sings my soul, my Saviour God, to Thee.
How great Thou art, how great Thou art!
Then sings my soul, my Saviour God, to Thee.
How great Thou art, how great Thou art!

When through the woods and forest glades I wander
And hear the birds sing sweetly in the trees;
When I look down from lofty mountain grandeur
And hear the brook and feel the gentle breeze,

And when I think that God, His Son not sparing,
Sent Him to die, I scarce can take it in;—
That on the Cross, my burden gladly bearing,
He bled and died to take away my sin.—

When Christ shall come with shout of acclamation
And take me home, what joy shall fill my heart!
Then I shall bow in humble adoration
And there proclaim, my God, how great Thou art!

Edward Hopper (1818–1888)

Jesus, Saviour, Pilot Me

In the nineteenth century one of the many missions established in New York City was called the Church of Sea and Land. Located in the harbor area, this church ministered to sailors from the many ocean liners that docked in the city. Edward Hopper, a Presbyterian minister, was pastor of that church in 1870 when he wrote the hymn "Jesus, Saviour, Pilot Me." In it he used language familiar to sailors—charts, compasses, the need for a competent pilot—to make spiritual truths more understandable, much as Jesus had done in his parables. The hymn first appeared anonymously in *The Sailor's Magazine* in 1871. John Gould (1822–1875), a music publisher, saw it in the magazine and composed the tune shortly before he himself set sail from New York. At the time he was in failing health, and he found that the words of the hymn expressed his need for a sure pilot over the tempestuous sea of his own life.

In 1880 Hopper was asked to write a hymn for an anniversary celebration of The Seamen's Friend Society in New York City. Instead he read "Jesus, Saviour, Pilot Me" publicly for the first time, acknowledging his authorship of the already well known hymn. He was delighted when most of those present could sing it from memory.

Hopper died sitting in his chair while composing a new hymn, this time on the subject of heaven. No doubt he heard Christ say to him, "Fear not, I will pilot thee."

Jesus, Saviour, pilot me
Over life's tempestuous sea.
Unknown waves before me roll,
Hiding rocks and treach'rous shoal.
Chart and compass came from Thee;
Jesus, Saviour, pilot me.

As a mother stills her child,
Thou canst hush the ocean wild;
Boist'rous waves obey Thy will
When Thou say'st to them, "Be still!"
Wondrous Sov'reign of the sea,
Jesus, Saviour, pilot me.

When at last I near the shore,
And the fearful breakers roar
'Twixt me and the peaceful rest,
Then, while leaning on Thy breast,
May I hear Thee say to me,
"Fear not, I will pilot thee."

Julia Ward Howe (1819–1910)

Battle Hymn of the Republic

One day early in the Civil War Julia Ward Howe, who lived in Washington, D.C., watched a parade of soldiers heading off to war. They were singing the popular song "John Brown's Body," named for the abolitionist who was hanged for his efforts to free the slaves. Howe's former pastor, visiting from Boston, was watching the parade with her. "Why don't you write something more uplifting to that tune?" he suggested. Later that night Howe awoke with words fully formed in her mind. Kenneth Osbeck in *101 Hymns Stories* reports her words: "I sprang out of bed and in the dimness found an old stump of a pen, which I remembered using the day before. I scrawled the verses almost without looking at the paper."

In 1862 Howe showed the poem to James T. Fields, editor of the *Atlantic Monthly*. He published it in his magazine under the title "The Battle Hymn of the Republic." Chaplain C. C. McCabe picked it up and taught it to his 122nd Ohio Volunteer Infantry. Soon the song spread to other units, and it became a rallying cry of patriotic feeling for the North during the war. Today its original purpose has long been forgotten, but it remains a popular national hymn.

Winston Churchill requested this hymn be sung at his funeral service in 1965. It also was sung at the inauguration of Lyndon Johnson in 1965 and at the memorial service of Robert Kennedy in 1968.

Julia Ward Howe, who was paid five dollars for her poem when it was published in the *Atlantic Monthly*, was descended from leaders of the Revolutionary War. Raised in a conservative Episcopal home, she became a champion of liberal humanitarian causes. She was actively opposed to slavery, crusaded for women's rights, and worked on trying to unite women of the world to strive for peace. She lectured and wrote extensively, raised four children, and never lost her belief in the presence of a personal God who controls human affairs.

Mine eyes have seen the glory
    of the coming of the Lord;
He is trampling out the vintage
    where the grapes of wrath are stored:
He hath loosed the fateful lightning
    of His terrible swift sword;
His truth is marching on.

Refrain
Glory! glory, hallelujah!
Glory! glory, hallelujah!
Glory! glory, hallelujah!
His truth is marching on.

I have seen Him in the watchfires
    of a hundred circling camps;
They have builded Him an altar
    in the evening dews and damps;

I can read His righteous sentence
    by the dim and flaring lamps;
His day is marching on.

He has sounded forth the trumpet
    that shall never sound retreat;
He is sifting out the hearts of men
    before His judgment seat.
O be swift, my soul, to answer Him!
    be jubilant, my feet!
Our God is marching on.

In the beauty of the lilies
    Christ was born across the sea,
With a glory in His bosom
    that transfigures you and me;
As He died to make men holy,
    let us die to make men free;
While God is marching on.

Mary Lathbury (1841–1913)

On the shores of Lake Chautauqua in western New York State, a conference center was established by Mary Lathbury and John Vincent (later a bishop of the Methodist Church and the man for whom I was named). Its purpose was to provide religious and cultural education for the American people. Ever since its founding in 1874 people have flocked to the Chautauqua Institution to hear leaders in religion, education, and the arts and to vacation on the shores of its picturesque lake.

Mary Lathbury became known as the "Poet Laureate and Saint of Chautauqua." She was both an artist and writer and was famous for her poetry, articles, and illustrations. In 1877 she wrote the following hymns especially for use at Chautauqua. They were put to music by William Sherwin (1826–1888), music director of the conference center. "Day Is Dying in the West" was inspired by the setting sun over Lake Chautauqua and was first sung by about two thousand people gathered on the shores of that lake for evening vespers. It has continued to be sung for vespers at Chautauqua ever since.

Day Is Dying in the West

Day is dying in the West,
    Heav'n is touching earth with rest;
Wait and worship while the night
    Sets her evening lamps alight
 Thro' all the sky.

Refrain
Holy, holy, holy, Lord God of Hosts!
Heav'n and earth are full of Thee!
Heav'n and earth are praising Thee,
 O Lord most high!

Lord of life, beneath the dome
    Of the universe, Thy home,
Gather us, who seek Thy face,
    To the fold of Thy embrace,
 For Thou art nigh.

While the deep'ning shadows fall,
    Heart of Love, enfolding all,

71

Thro' the glory and the grace
　　Of the stars that veil Thy face
　Our hearts ascend.

When forever from our sight
　　Pass the stars, the day, the night,
Lord of angels, on our eyes
　　Let eternal morning rise
　And shadows end!

Break Thou the Bread of Life

Break Thou the bread of life,
　　Dear Lord, to me,
As Thou didst break the loaves
　　Beside the sea.
Beyond the sacred page
　　I seek Thee, Lord;
My spirit pants for Thee,
　　O living Word!

Bless Thou the Truth, dear Lord,
　　This day to me,

As Thou didst bless the bread
    By Galilee.
Then shall all bondage cease,
    All fetters fall,
And I shall find my peace,
    My All in All.

Martin Luther (1483–1546)

A Mighty Fortress Is Our God

Martin Luther, the father of the Protestant Reformation, was also the founder of congregational singing. While he wrote more than one hundred hymns, by far his best and most famous is "A Mighty Fortress Is Our God." Luther was born in 1483 in Eisleben, Germany, to a poor mining family. He was greatly talented in music, both in singing and in playing the flute and lute. To Luther music was a "gift and a grace of God." Despite the objections of his father, who wanted him to be a lawyer, Luther was ordained a priest in the Roman Catholic Church in 1507, and the following year he began teaching philosophy and theology at Wittenberg University.

Martin Luther struggled against some of the beliefs and practices of the Roman Catholic Church, and he outlined his dissatisfaction in the famous Ninety-five Theses that he nailed to the door of the Wittenberg church in 1517. These struggles culminated in his excommunication in 1520, a traumatic event that brought new direction to the church in Germany. Luther translated the Bible into German so people could read it themselves. He also wrote hymns in German so that congregational singing would become a vital part of the worship service. Luther believed that having both hymns and Bibles in their native language would help people claim religious expression as their own.

In 1524 the first Protestant hymnal was published in Wittenberg. Four of its eight hymns were written by Luther. In the next twenty years more than one hundred collections of hymns were printed, and for many of those hymns Luther had written both the words and the music.

"A Mighty Fortress," often called the "Battle Hymn of the Reformation," was written in 1527 during a time of enormous pressure and suffering for Luther. It was based on Psalm 46: "God is our refuge and strength, a very present help in trouble." At the time Luther was nearly penniless but felt obliged to offer hospitality to the many visitors who came to his door. He suffered from painful digestive disorders, bouts of depression, and severe headaches. He almost died from the plague that killed several of his close friends. In spite of these difficult times, he found help in looking to God as his fortress and strength. All of us, no matter what the circumstances of our lives, can say with Luther, "A mighty Fortress is our God, a Bulwark never failing."

A mighty Fortress is our God,
    A Bulwark never failing;
Our Helper He, amid the flood
    Of mortal ills prevailing.
For still our ancient foe
    Doth seek to work us woe;
His craft and power are great,
    And, armed with cruel hate,
On earth is not his equal.

Did we in our own strength confide,
    Our striving would be losing,
Were not the right Man on our side,
    The Man of God's own choosing.
Dost ask who that may be?
    Christ Jesus, it is He;
Lord Sabaoth, His name,
    From age to age the same
And He must win the battle.

And though this world, with devils filled,
    Should threaten to undo us.
We will not fear, for God hath willed
    His truth to triumph through us.
The prince of darkness grim—
    We tremble not for him.
His rage we can endure,
    For, lo, his doom is sure;
One little word shall fell him.

That word above all earthly powers,
    No thanks to them, abideth;
The Spirit and the gifts are ours
    Through Him who with us sideth.
Let goods and kindred go,
    This mortal life also.
The body they may kill;
    God's truth abideth still.
His kingdom is forever.

Henry F. Lyte (1793–1847)

Abide with Me

Henry Francis Lyte remained totally obscure until after his death. Now a plaque in Westminster Abbey honors him as one of England's greatest. That tribute was for a single poem, "Abide with Me," which lay forgotten for fifteen years after its author's death before becoming one of the major hymns of the church.

Henry Lyte was born in Scotland, orphaned at an early age, and educated at Trinity College in Ireland. He was a priest in the Church of England, and for the last twenty-three years of his life he ministered in the poor fishing village of Lower Brixham, Devonshire, England. He was loved by the people for his gentle and winsome ways and tireless devotion to their welfare; developing a Sunday school of seven hundred children was one of his many accomplishments. He was a man of great faith and courage; even when tuberculosis ravaged his body he commented, "It is better to wear out than rust out."

By 1847 Lyte's health had deteriorated to such a point that his church decided to send him to a warmer climate to recover his strength. He preached his last sermon on Sunday, September 4, 1847, and spent that afternoon walking by the sea, watching the sun splash colors of crimson and gold across the sky as it fell below the horizon. He returned to his room and wrote a poem, "Abide with Me, Fast Falls the Eventide." Lyte had written many poems in his life, but he always wanted to write something that would outlast him. He gave this poem to a relative and the next day set sail for Italy. When he reached Nice, France, he was too weak to continue, and he died there on November 20, 1847.

In 1850 the poem was put into a book entitled *Lyte's Remains*. William Henry Monk (1823–1889), a well-known organist and hymn writer in England, was editing a hymnbook in 1861 when he came across Lyte's poem and discovered it was not set to music. He was deeply moved by the words, and it is said he composed a tune for them in half an hour. It is considered his best composition.

In an earlier poem Lyte had expressed the desire to write "some simple strain, some spirit-moving lay, some sparkle of the soul that still might live when I passed to clay. . . ." That desire was realized in the hymn "Abide with Me." Both Queen Elizabeth II and her mother chose this hymn to open their wedding ceremonies, and it was also sung at the funeral of King George V on January 28, 1936. In a scene that would have touched Lyte's heart, Edith Cavel, an English nurse, sang this hymn on October 12, 1915, as she faced a German firing squad for helping Allied soldiers escape from German-occupied Belgium.

Abide with me! Fast falls the eventide.
The darkness deepens: Lord with me abide!
When other helpers fail and comforts flee,
Help of the helpless, oh, abide with me!

Swift to its close ebbs out life's little day.
Earth's joys grow dim; its glories pass away.
Change and decay in all around I see;
O Thou who changest not, abide with me!

I need Thy presence ev'ry passing hour.
What but Thy grace can foil the tempter's pow'r?
Who, like thyself, my guide and stay can be?
Thro' clouds and sunshine, oh, abide with me!

I fear no foe, with Thee at hand to bless;
Ills have no weight, and tears no bitterness.
Where is death's sting? Where, grave, thy victory?
I triumph still if Thou abide with me.

Hold Thou Thy cross before my closing eyes;
Shine thro' the gloom, and point me to the skies.
Heav'n's morning breaks, and earth's vain shadows flee!
In life, in death, O Lord, abide with me!

Civilla D. Martin (1869–1948)

God Will Take Care of You

The remark of a young boy to his father was the inspiration for the popular hymn "God Will Take Care of You." The incident occurred in 1904 while Stillman and Civilla Martin were spending several weeks at the Practical Bible Training School in Lestershire, New York, where Stillman was helping to prepare a songbook. Stillman was a Baptist evangelist and had accepted a preaching engagement some distance away, but that Sunday morning Civilla became seriously ill. Stillman's first thought was to cancel his engagement and remain at home with her, when their nine-year-old son reportedly said to him, "Father, don't you think that if God wants you to preach today, he will take care of Mother while you are away?"

Properly convinced by these words, Stillman kept his commitment. Civilla, though ill, overheard her son's words to his father, and later that day she jotted down the text to this hymn. When her husband returned, excited by the overwhelming spiritual renewal that occurred in church that morning, he found Civilla much improved. After she showed him the hymn text he sat down immediately at his small reed organ and composed the melody. It is sung today exactly as the Martins wrote it ninety years ago.

Civilla Martin had studied music prior to her marriage and wrote several other songs, the most notable being "His Eye Is on the Sparrow." She aided her husband in his many evangelistic meetings and collaborated with him on many other hymns, but "God Will Take Care of You" is their most lasting work.

Be not dismayed whate'er betide;
God will take care of you.
Beneath His wings of love abide;
God will take care of you.

Refrain
God will take care of you,
Thro' ev'ry day, O'er all the way.
He will take care of you;
God will take care of you.

Thro' days of toil when heart doth fail;
God will take care of you;
When dangers fierce your path assail,
God will take care of you.

All you may need He will provide;
God will take care of you.

81

Nothing you ask will be denied;
    God will take care of you.

No matter what may be the test,
    God will take care of you.
Lean, weary one, upon His breast;
    God will take care of you.

George Matheson (1842–1906)

O Love That Wilt Not Let Me Go

Some people not only rise above adversity but, through it, become strong and creative. Such a person was George Matheson. Totally blind by the time he was eighteen, he nevertheless became one of Scotland's best-known preachers, serving as pastor of a two-thousand-member church in Edinburgh. His sister assisted him in his pastoral duties and even learned Greek, Latin, and Hebrew to help him in his scholarly pursuits. Matheson had developed an extraordinary memory and used it in preparing his weekly sermon. After dictating the sermon to his sister, she would read it back to him twice. That was all he needed to memorize it, and on Sunday he preached it word for word, exactly as he had written it.

"O Love That Wilt Not Let Me Go" was written June 6, 1882, his sister's wedding day. Matheson gives this account of its birth, reported in *Lyric Religion* by Augustine Smith (New York: Appleton-Century-Crofts, 1931): "Something happened to me which was known only to myself, and which caused me the most severe mental suffering. The hymn was the fruit of that suffering. . . . I had the impression rather of having it dictated to me by some inward voice. . . . I am quite sure that the whole work was completed in five minutes. . . . It never received at my hands any retouching correction."

Some have speculated that his sister's wedding day rekindled memories of his fiancée, who had broken their engagement when she learned that Matheson would be totally blind. Whatever the cause of his mental suffering, however, he truly believed that a loving God would never abandon him.

The tune was written by Albert Peace (1844–1912).

O Love that wilt not let me go,
I rest my weary soul in Thee.
I give Thee back the life I owe,
That in Thine ocean depths its flow
May richer, fuller be.

O Light that followest all my way,
I yield my flick'ring torch to Thee.
My heart restores its borrowed ray,
That in Thy sunshine's blaze its day
May brighter, fairer be.

O Joy that seekest me through pain,
I cannot close my heart to Thee.
I trace the rainbow through the rain,
And feel the promise is not vain
That morn shall tearless be.

O Cross that liftest up my head,
I dare not ask to fly from Thee.
I lay in dust life's glory dead,
And from the ground there blossoms red
Life that shall endless be.

C. Austin Miles (1868–1946)

In the Garden

One day in 1912 Austin Miles, editor of a music publishing firm in Philadelphia, was sitting in his study reading the account of Mary visiting Jesus' tomb on Easter morning (John 20). He used his imagination to put himself in that garden by the tomb, seeing Mary first distraught and then filled with joy at recognizing Jesus. He felt he was there himself, living the events that followed. Miles later recounted what happened next. "I awakened in full light, gripping the Bible, with muscles tense and nerves vibrating. Under the inspiration of this vision, I wrote as quickly as the words could be formed the poem exactly as it has since appeared. That same evening, I wrote the music" (George W. Sanville, *Forty Gospel Hymn Stories* [Winona Lake, IN: Rodeheaver-Hall-Mack, 1943]).

This hymn is a personal ballad, written from Mary's point of view. It gained a place as one of America's best-loved gospel songs through its use at Billy Sunday crusades and other evangelistic meetings.

One of the reasons for this hymn's popularity, I believe, is its beautiful image of Jesus caring for each of us personally. In a book entitled *A Window to Heaven* (Grand Rapids: Zondervan, 1992),

Dr. Diane M. Komp, a pediatric oncologist, tells the stories of children with cancer whose spiritual experiences help them cope with life in the face of death. One of her patients, a young man named Tom, contracted cancer in high school and watched it progress to the point where he became a quadriplegic. As Dr. Komp writes, "In this condition, Tom was discharged to his home on his twentieth birthday. When I visited him, he was able to move only his head and neck, and required total nursing care. When we were alone, he told me of a vision that came to him while he was meditating.

"He saw himself in a beautiful garden and saw a man there, seated on a bench. The man's fingers were like roses, and he walked with Tom in the garden and talked to him. The man touched him, and Tom reported that he moved in his bed for the first time in months. He did not want to leave the garden or the man's presence, but his companion went ahead and told him that he could not come with him yet.

"I asked Tom if he knew who the man was. He said, 'I *know* it was Jesus.'

"I could tell from his eyes that he was afraid that I would not believe him. Thinking of the images he described, I thought for sure that he must be recreating the old Gospel hymn 'In the Garden.'

"Tom was confused by my question, because he had never heard of the hymn. When I sang it for him, he did not recognize the melody, but was excited because he recognized in the words the parallel image to his vision. Two days later, he told his parents that he would not live through the night and died peacefully in his sleep."

God uses hymns to touch us in ways, both large and small, that are little short of miraculous.

I come to the garden alone,
> While the dew is still on the roses;
And the voice I hear,
> Falling on my ear,
The Son of God discloses.

Refrain
And He walks with me,
> and He talks with me,
And He tells me I am His own;
And the joy we share as we tarry there,
> None other has ever known.

He speaks, and the sound of His voice
> Is so sweet the birds hush their singing,
And the melody
> That He gave to me
Within my heart is ringing.

I'd stay in the garden with Him
    Tho' the night around me be falling,
But He bids me go;
    Thru the voice of woe,
His voice to me is calling.

Joseph Mohr (1792–1848)

Silent Night, Holy Night

The story of "Silent Night" is a familiar one. The year was 1818. As Christmas approached in the small village of Oberndorf, located in one of the valleys high in the Tyrolian Alps of Austria, a parish priest prepared for the traditional Christmas Eve mass. Unfortunately, the church's organ was broken, and that meant he had to find a song that would not require organ accompaniment. A Christmas service without music was unthinkable to the people of the Tyrol, for music was vital to their lives. To them music was like breathing.

Father Mohr decided to write his own song. He jotted down the words and gave them to Franz Gruber (1787–1863), his organist and the village schoolteacher. Gruber was excited by the words, for he had long felt the perfect Christmas carol had yet to be written. On Christmas Eve Mohr and Gruber sang the new song, accompanied by Gruber's guitar. The church choir, in four-part harmony, joined in on the last phrase of each stanza.

The carol was never intended for use beyond the village, but, as in the case of so many other hymns, a series of little events brought it to the world's attention. Karl Mauracher, well-known organ maker, finally arrived to repair the Oberndorf organ. He took a copy of the new hymn with him when he left and sang and played it in all the towns he visited. The song soon became a popular Tyrolean folk song. A singing group, the Strasser family, sang it at a fair in Leipzig in 1831, and other groups included it in their concerts as well.

"Silent Night" was first published anonymously in 1831 in a German hymnal. In 1854 Franz Gruber wrote the story behind its writing, and that same year it was sung before Emperor Frederick Wilhelm IV by the choir of the Imperial Church in Berlin. The emperor was so impressed that he ordered it be given the most prominent spot in future religious programs. German immigrants brought the carol to America, where it was first published in the Methodist hymnal in 1849. In 1863 John Young, Episcopal bishop of Florida, translated it into English, and it is his version we sing today.

The secret of the carol's success is its simplicity of style—a perfect blending of words and music. That simplicity came out of need, for no organ or piano was available for embellishment.

Today this hymn has been translated into all major languages and is considered the world's favorite Christmas carol. Franz Gruber finally got his perfect Christmas song.

Silent night, holy night,
All is calm, all is bright
Round yon virgin mother and child.
Holy infant so tender and mild,
Sleep in heavenly peace,
Sleep in heavenly peace.

Silent night, holy night,
Shepherds quake, at the sight,
Glories stream from heaven afar,
Heavenly hosts sing alleluia,
Christ the Saviour is born,
Christ the Saviour is born.

Silent night, holy night,
Son of God, love's pure light
Radiant beams from thy holy face,
With the dawn of redeeming grace,
Jesus Lord, at thy birth
Jesus Lord, at thy birth.

John Newton (1725–1807)

Amazing Grace

"Amazing Grace" was written by an obscure Anglican minister in his midfifties, but it reflects the life of a truly remarkable man.

John Newton lost his mother when he was six, dropped out of school to go to sea on his father's ship at age eleven, and later became a slave trader along the coast of West Africa. By the time he became captain of his own slave ship, he was a confirmed atheist, living the wild and reckless life of a brutal and hardened seaman.

On March 10, 1748, while returning from Africa to England, a severe storm threatened the ship. Perhaps it was the Scripture verses his mother had taught him as a child, perhaps it was the book he had picked up, *The Imitation of Christ* by Thomas à Kempis, or perhaps it was a sudden realization of possible death. For whatever reason, John Newton had a profound spiritual experience that stormy night.

The voyage was completed safely, and Newton continued piloting his slave ship, but he was a changed man. He became more humane in his treatment of the slaves and even held a church service for his crew every Sunday. Six years later, feeling convinced of the evils of slavery, he took a land job in Liverpool, England, checking ships for contraband.

In his midthirties he felt called to the ministry, and at age thirty-nine he was ordained an Anglican priest. Since Newton had had no university training, the bishop was reluctant to appoint him to a parish, but an influential patron intervened on his behalf. He was given a church in Olney, a small factory town, and it was there that he wrote "Amazing Grace." It is an autobiographical hymn, describing the power of God to change a person's life completely.

John Newton introduced hymn singing to his church. When his congregation had sung all the available hymns, Newton began writing his own. In 1879 he coauthored the Olney hymnal, one of England's earliest hymnbooks. It was used in England and America for more than one hundred years. In that hymnal was another one of Newton's beautiful hymns, "Glorious Things of Thee Are Spoken," a testimony to God's constant protection.

In his later years Newton was rector at the influential St. Mary Woolnoth church in London. He campaigned vigorously for the abolition of the slave trade, and he never ceased to wonder at the amazing grace that had redirected his life.

The tune of "Amazing Grace" is purported to be from an early Protestant hymn tune called *New Britain*, but slight changes in the melody have been made over two centuries. This is a well-beloved tune, popularized by musicians and singers the world over.

Amazing grace! how sweet the sound!
That saved a wretch like me!
I once was lost, but now am found;
Was blind, but now I see.

'Twas grace that taught my heart to fear,
And grace my fears relieved.
How precious did that grace appear
The hour I first believed!

Thro' many dangers, toils and snares
I have already come.
'Tis grace hath bro't me safe thus far,
And grace will lead me home.

When we've been there ten thousand years,
Bright, shining as the sun,
We've no less days to sing God's praise
Than when we first begun.

Ray Palmer (1808–1887)

My Faith Looks Up to Thee

Ray Palmer was born in Rhode Island, the son of a judge who taught him at home throughout his elementary school years. Because of the family's financial difficulties Ray left school at thirteen and became a clerk in a dry goods store in Boston. After a religious conversion at Park Street Congregational Church he went back to school, graduating from Andover Academy and later Yale University.

With his teaching credentials Palmer secured a part-time position in New York City. One night in 1830, shortly after graduating from college, he sat alone in his room reading. At twenty-two he felt lonely, isolated, and frustrated as he contemplated his future. He was so moved by the German poem he was reading that he translated it into English, adding four new verses. These verses were not intended to be a hymn; they were simply words for private devotions. He copied them into a small notebook that he carried in his pocket and read them periodically.

Two years later on a street in Boston, Palmer ran into a friend, Lowell Mason, a renowned musician and music publisher. Mason asked if he had any good texts he could use in a new hymnal he was compiling. Palmer showed him his notebook. Mason was interested in the verses written in New York two years earlier, so they stepped into a store, where he copied them onto a piece of paper.

Several days later Mason wrote to Palmer and said, "Mr. Palmer, you may live many years and do many good things, but I think you will be best known to posterity as the author of 'My Faith Looks Up to Thee.'" Ray Palmer did become an outstanding preacher and pastor, but he is known today for this one hymn that many have said is the finest American hymn ever written.

The tune was composed by Lowell Mason (1792–1872), who wrote tunes for more than seven hundred hymn texts, among them "Joy to the World," "O Day of Rest and Gladness," "Nearer, My God, to Thee," and "When I Survey the Wondrous Cross." He compiled more than eighty songbooks, founded the Boston Academy of Music, and introduced the use of music into public school curriculums. Mason was awarded the Doctor of Music degree from New York University, only the second such degree awarded in the United States at that time.

That chance meeting on a Boston street corner in 1832 has given us one of the world's most cherished hymns.

My faith looks up to Thee,
Thou Lamb of Calvary,

Saviour divine!
Now hear me while I pray;
Take all my guilt away.
Oh, let me from this day
Be wholly Thine!

May Thy rich grace impart
Strength to my fainting heart,
My zeal inspire.
As Thou hast died for me,
Oh, may my love to Thee
Pure, warm, and changeless be,
A living fire!

While life's dark maze I tread,
And griefs around me spread,
Be Thou my Guide.
Bid darkness turn to day;
Wipe sorrow's tears away;
Nor let me ever stray
From Thee aside!

When ends life's transient dream,
When death's cold, sullen stream

Shall o'er me roll,
Blest Saviour, then in love
Fear and distrust remove.
Oh, bear me safe above,
A ransomed soul!

Edward Perronet (1726–1792)

All Hail the Power of Jesus' Name

Called by some the national anthem of Christendom, "All Hail the Power of Jesus' Name" is one of the most inspiring and triumphant hymns in the English language. The words suggest royal pageantry, and the images emphasize the majesty and power of Christ.

The hymn was written by Edward Perronet, a minister first in the Anglican Church and later with the evangelical movement led by George Whitefield and John and Charles Wesley. Perronet was born in Sundridge, Kent, England, in 1726 and was descended from a distinguished French Huguenot family who had fled from France because of religious persecution. Edward himself encountered trouble during the 1740s and 1750s because of his participation in the Wesleyan evangelical movement.

Perronet was a strong-minded and free-spirited man. He broke with the Wesleys at one point over the issue of who could administer the sacraments. Also, he wanted the Wesleyan movement to separate from the Anglican Church and become a new denomination, a vision not shared by John and Charles Wesley. However, Perronet also had tremendous loyalty and respect for the Wesley brothers, evidenced in the following incident. John Wesley announced one day that Edward Perronet would preach at the next worship service. Reluctant to preach in the presence of the great man but not wanting to go against his wishes, Perronet mounted the pulpit and announced that he would deliver the finest sermon ever preached. He then proceeded to read the entire Sermon on the Mount from the Bible.

The original version of "All Hail the Power," which had fourteen stanzas, underwent many alterations. Most American hymnals use the version by the Reverend John Rippon (1751–1836), an English Baptist minister.

The hymn's original tune, which still is used extensively throughout Great Britain and Europe, was composed by William Shrubsole. The most popular tune in America, the "Coronation," was composed by Oliver Holden (1765–1844), a Massachusetts carpenter, singing teacher, and musician.

This hymn, proclaiming the power of the name of Jesus, has been used by many to gain strength in uncertain circumstances.

One story is attributed to E. P. Scott, a missionary to India. Way-laid by hostile tribesmen one day, he pulled out his violin and began to play and sing this hymn. When he came to the stanza "Let every kindred, every tribe," the natives lowered their spears and let him pass. God can reach our hearts and minds today through the words of this ancient hymn.

All hail the pow'r of Jesus' name!
Let angels prostrate fall.
Bring forth the royal diadem,
And crown Him Lord of all.
Bring forth the royal diadem,
And crown Him Lord of all.

Ye chosen seed of Israel's race,
Ye ransomed from the Fall,
Hail Him who saves you by His grace,
And crown Him Lord of all.
Hail Him who saves you by His grace,
And crown Him Lord of all.

Let ev'ry kindred, ev'ry tribe,
On this terrestrial ball,
To Him all majesty ascribe,

And crown Him Lord of all.
To Him all majesty ascribe,
And crown Him Lord of all.

Oh, that with yonder sacred throng
We at His feet may fall!
We'll join the everlasting song,
And crown Him Lord of all.
We'll join the everlasting song,
And crown Him Lord of all.

Adelaide A. Pollard (1862–1934)

Have Thine Own Way, Lord

Adelaide Pollard was experiencing great inner turmoil in her life in 1902. Although she was a teacher, she had dreamed of becoming a missionary, but her poor health had prevented this dream from being realized. One night she attended a prayer meeting. Someone at that meeting prayed, "Lord, it doesn't matter what you bring into our lives, just have your own way with us." Those words, *have your own way,* stuck in Adelaide Pollard's mind, and that night she wrote the text of this hymn. It was put to music in 1907 by George Stebbins (1846–1945), composer, publisher, and well-known gospel song leader with evangelists D. L. Moody and Ira Sankey.

Years later, when she was quite old, Pollard had an experience that confirmed God's guidance in the writing of this hymn. William J. Reynolds describes it in his book, *Songs of Glory:* "[Pollard] entered a Christian bookstore, in Philadelphia, seeking some study material. The young clerk who helped her mentioned her own conversion experience. The clerk told of the minister's message, which spoke so directly to her, and the singing of 'Have Thine Own Way, Lord,' which led her to accept Christ. At the mention of the hymn, the old lady's face brightened and she told how the hymn came into being. . . .

"After the old lady finished telling the story to the sales clerk, her eyes filled with tears and she said, 'I wrote that hymn many years ago, never dreaming how much God would use it for a blessing in other lives.'"

"Have Thine Own Way, Lord" has been a blessing in many lives, including my own.

> Have Thine own way, Lord!
>   Have Thine own way!
> Thou art the Potter;
>   I am the clay.

Mould me and make me
    After Thy will,
While I am waiting,
    Yielded and still.

Have Thine own way, Lord!
    Have Thine own way!
Search me and try me,
    Master, today!
Whiter than snow, Lord,
    Wash me just now.
As in Thy presence
    Humbly I bow.

Have Thine own way, Lord!
    Have Thine own way!
Wounded and weary,
    Help me, I pray!
Power—all power—
    Surely is thine!
Touch me and heal me,
    Savior divine!

Have Thine own way, Lord!
    Have Thine own way!
Hold o'er my being
    Absolute sway!
Fill with Thy Spirit
    Till all shall see
Christ only, always,
    Living in me!

Elizabeth P. Prentiss (1818–1878)

More Love to Thee

Like many hymns, "More Love to Thee" was born out of great personal sorrow. In the 1850s Elizabeth Prentiss, a frail woman who suffered intense physical pain and was an invalid most of her life, experienced the deaths of two of her young children. In trying to come to terms with her loss, she studied the story of Jacob and how God had met his need in time of sorrow. She began to experience God's closeness and to find comfort in his love for her. Then one day in 1856, in a moment of inspiration, she wrote the words for the hymn "More Love to Thee." Without showing it to anyone she put it away, as though the writing of it was all she needed.

Elizabeth Prentiss had been an author since childhood. At sixteen she contributed both prose and poetry to youth magazines, and one of her later books, *Stepping Heavenward,* sold more than three hundred thousand copies in the United States alone. In 1845 she married Dr. George Prentiss, a Presbyterian minister who later became a professor at Union Theological Seminary in New York City.

Thirteen years after writing the poem "More Love to Thee," she finally showed it to her husband. He encouraged her to have it published in a leaflet and distributed to their friends. One of the leaflets found its way to a Cincinnati, Ohio, businessman named William Doane (1832–1915), whose avocation was writing gospel music. Doane had started composing after a serious illness at the urging of Fanny Crosby, the noted hymn writer for whose texts Doane wrote many tunes. The hymn as we know it today was published in 1870 and was used frequently in the evangelistic crusades of D. L. Moody and Ira Sankey. Doane also wrote tunes for "I Am Thine, O Lord," "Pass Me Not, O Gentle Savior," "Rescue the Perishing," and "To God Be the Glory."

More love to Thee, O Christ,
    More love to Thee!

Hear Thou the prayer I make
    On bended knee.
This is my earnest plea:
    More love, O Christ, to Thee;
 More love to Thee,
 More love to Thee!

Once earthly joy I craved,
    Sought peace and rest.
Now Thee alone I seek;
    Give what is best.
This all my prayer shall be:
 More love, O Christ, to Thee;
 More love to Thee,
 More love to Thee!

Then shall my latest breath
    Whisper Thy praise.
This be the parting cry
    My heart shall raise;
This still my prayer shall be:
 More love, O Christ, to Thee;
 More love to Thee,
 More love to Thee!

Daniel C. Roberts (1841–1907)

God of Our Fathers

In 1876 the American people were gearing up to celebrate the one hundredth anniversary of the signing of the Declaration of Independence. Daniel Roberts, rector of a small Episcopal church in Brandon, Vermont, decided to write a hymn that expressed the belief that God had guided our nation in the past and would do so in the future. At the Fourth of July celebration in his rural church, "God of Our Fathers" was sung for the first time. The congregation did not know that its minister had written the hymn.

In the late 1880s Roberts submitted his hymn anonymously to the committee revising the Episcopal hymnal. After it was accepted, Roberts confirmed his identity as the author. Prior to its publication, "God of Our Fathers" was chosen as the hymn for the centennial celebration of the adoption of the United States Constitution in 1889. George W. Warren (1828–1902), organist of St. Thomas Episcopal Church in New York City, was commissioned to write a new tune for the hymn. The dramatic trumpet lines before each verse gave it a distinctive patriotic flare and inspirational quality.

For Roberts, who had served as a private in the Civil War, this hymn was his one literary achievement. While it did not become immediately popular, today it is included in all major hymnbooks and continues to be sung at national celebrations across this land. Roberts went on to be pastor of St. Paul's Church in Concord, New Hampshire, where he served with distinction for thirty years.

God of our fathers, whose almighty hand
Leads forth in beauty all the starry band
Of shining worlds in splendor through the skies,
Our grateful songs before Thy throne arise.

Thy love divine hath led us in the past.
In this free land by Thee our lot is cast.
Be Thou our Ruler, Guardian, Guide and Stay,
Thy Word our law, Thy paths our chosen way.

From war's alarms, from deadly pestilence,
Be Thy strong arm our ever sure defense.
Thy true religion in our hearts increase;
Thy bounteous goodness nourish us in peace.

Refresh Thy people on their toilsome way.
Lead us from night to neverending day.

Fill all our lives with love and grace divine;
And glory, laud, and praise be ever Thine.

Joseph Scriven (1819–1886)

What a Friend We Have in Jesus

Perhaps no other hymn grows out of the author's own personal heartache the way "What a Friend We Have in Jesus" does. It is also a glowing testimony to the belief that it is Jesus Christ who enables us to bear all the griefs and tragedies we may ever experience.

Born in Dublin, Ireland, Joseph Scriven planned to follow in his father's footsteps and enter military service, but poor health kept him from that dream. He later came under the influence of the Plymouth Brethren, which estranged him from his family, but his engagement to a beautiful young woman gave his life new meaning. The night before their wedding, however, she accidentally drowned. Despondent, he decided to emigrate to Canada, and eventually he settled near Port Hope, Ontario, where he became a tutor for a family named Pengelly.

In Canada Scriven devoted himself tirelessly to caring for the sick and needy. Some said his life was guided totally by the Sermon on the Mount. He lived in poverty, donating his possessions and most of his earnings to others who, he said, needed them more than he did. In 1855 he was engaged again, but before they could be married his fiancée died suddenly. Two years later he wrote the words for this hymn. It is said that he wrote it to comfort his mother, who was ill in Ireland, but I suspect he wrote it to encourage himself as well. It was never intended for publication, but a friend who chanced to see a scratched-up copy by Scriven's bedside had it included in a collection of Scriven's poems published in 1869. Later Ira Sankey printed it in his *Gospel Hymns Number One*. Scriven's later years were lived in increasingly poor health, loss of income, and periods of despondency. He died by drowning at the age of seventy-seven, an ironic end for a man whose life was beset by tragedy.

On a highway near Port Hope, by the shores of Lake Ontario, stands a monument with this inscription: "Four miles north, in Pengelly's Cemetery, lies the philanthropist and author of the great masterpiece, written at Port Hope, 1857." This inscription is followed by the stanzas of "What a Friend We Have in Jesus." It is a fitting tribute to one whose pain-filled life brought continued assurance that Jesus was indeed his friend.

What a Friend we have in Jesus,
    All our sins and griefs to bear!

What a privilege to carry
    Ev'rything to God in pray'r!
Oh, what peace we often forfeit,
    Oh, what needless pain we bear,
All because we do not carry
    Ev'rything to God in pray'r!

Have we trials and temptations?
    Is there trouble anywhere?
We should never be discouraged;
    Take it to the Lord in pray'r.
Can we find a friend so faithful
    Who will all our sorrows share?
Jesus knows our ev'ry weakness;
    Take it to the Lord in pray'r.

Are we weak and heavy laden,
    Cumbered with a load of care?
Precious Saviour, still our Refuge!
    Take it to the Lord in pray'r.
Do thy friends despise, forsake thee?
    Take it to the Lord in pray'r.
In His arms He'll take and shield thee;
    Thou wilt find a solace there.

Edmund H. Sears (1810–1876)

It Came upon the Midnight Clear

In 1849, when "It Came upon the Midnight Clear" was written, the country was in the midst of social upheaval. The gold rush was under way in California, the industrial revolution was transforming life in the East, and the issues that would lead us into the Civil War a decade later were already causing tensions between the North and South.

The hymn's author, Edmund Sears, was aware of these and other problems facing the nation, as he pastored a Unitarian church in Wayland, Massachusetts. They were on his heart as he wrote the text for this carol, evident in such references as "the weary world," "beneath life's crushing load," and "its sad and lonely plains." Although there is no mention of Christ in this hymn about his birth, the hymn does challenge us to listen to the message the angels brought and that Christ taught. This hymn is one of the first carols ever written by an American writer and one of the first with a social message, "Peace on the earth, good-will toward men."

The tune was written in 1850 by an American musician, Richard Willis (1819–1900), a music critic for the *New York Herald*

Tribune and other newspapers and a friend of Felix Mendelssohn, whom he met while studying in Germany. The tune was originally written for another hymn but found its perfect match when joined with this text.

Too great a familiarity with this hymn may keep us from hearing its message, which is as relevant today as it was when it was written. Our broken world still needs to hear the message the angels sing.

It came upon the midnight clear,
That glorious song of old,
From angels bending near the earth
To touch their harps of gold.
"Peace on the earth, good-will to men,
From heav'n's all-gracious King."
The world in solemn stillness lay
To hear the angels sing.

Still thro' the cloven skies they come,
With peaceful wings unfurled,
And still their heav'nly music floats
O'er all the weary world.
Above its sad and lowly plains
They bend on hov'ring wing,

And ever o'er its babel sounds
The blessed angels sing.

And ye, beneath life's crushing load,
Whose forms are bending low,
Who toil along the climbing way
With painful steps and slow,
Look up! For glad and golden hours
Come swiftly on the wing.
Oh, rest beside the weary road
And hear the angels sing.

For lo, the days are hast'ning on,
By prophet bards foretold,
When with the ever circling years
Come round the age of gold;
When peace shall over all the earth
Its ancient splendors fling,
And the whole world give back the song
Which now the angels sing.

Samuel F. Smith (1808–1895)

My Country, 'Tis of Thee

Lowell Mason, the noted music educator and hymn tune writer, was a good friend of Samuel F. Smith, who in 1832 was a student at Andover Theological Seminary. Because Smith was a linguist (he could converse fluently in fifteen languages), Mason asked him to look through a book of German songs to see if any of them would be suitable for Mason's children's choirs.

As Smith flipped through the pages, he came upon a song entitled "God Save Our Native Land." Moved by the patriotic nature of the German song, he thought, "We need a hymn like that for our country." He took a scrap of paper, and in thirty minutes "My Country, 'Tis of Thee" was born. It was first sung in a park in Boston the following Fourth of July by Lowell Mason's children's choir from the Park Street Congregational Church, and its author was sitting in the audience.

Samuel Smith went on to become one of the great Baptist preachers of his day. In addition to serving several large churches, he composed more than one hundred hymns, compiled a widely used hymnal, and traveled around the world visiting mission fields. His patriotic hymn, written when he was only twenty-four years of age, remains his best-known achievement. Considered our unofficial national anthem, the first four verses remain exactly as he wrote them. A fifth verse was removed because it contained strong anti-British sentiment.

The tune is Britain's national anthem, sung as "God Save the King" or "Queen." It also is a national song for nineteen other nations, who use it with their own patriotic verses.

My country, 'tis of thee,
Sweet land of liberty,
   Of thee I sing:
Land where my fathers died,
Land of the Pilgrims' pride.
From ev'ry mountainside
Let freedom ring!

My native country, thee,
Land of the noble, free,
   Thy name I love.
I love thy rocks and rills,
Thy woods and templed hill;
My heart with rapture thrills
Like that above.

Let music swell the breeze,
And ring from all the trees
    Sweet freedom's song.
Let mortal tongues awake;
Let all that breathe partake;
Let rocks their silence break,
The sound prolong.

Our fathers' God to Thee,
Author of liberty,
    To Thee we sing.
Long may our land be bright
With freedom's holy light;
Protect us by Thy might,
Great God, our King!

Horatio G. Spafford (1828–1888)

It Is Well with My Soul

A great personal tragedy sent Horatio Spafford deep into the heart of his faith, and he emerged able to state, "It is well with my soul." Let me tell you the story.

In the late 1860s Horatio Spafford, a successful Chicago businessman, experienced the loss of his son and then saw the great Chicago fire of 1871 destroy most of the real estate investments he had made on the shore of Lake Michigan. To recover from these losses and to assist his friend D. L. Moody in an evangelical crusade in England, Spafford planned a European vacation for his wife and four daughters. Because of last-minute business problems, he had to delay his departure, but he sent his family on the SS *Ville de Havre* as planned. On November 22, 1873, their ship was struck by an English vessel and sank in less than twelve minutes. Several days later Spafford received the following cable from his wife who had been rescued and taken to Wales: "Saved alone." His four daughters were lost at sea.

On the voyage to join his wife, the ship's captain called him up to the deck one night and told him, "This is the area where the ship went down." Spafford stood there for some time staring at the ocean. Then he went to his cabin and wrote, "It Is Well with My Soul."

Spafford later gave the words to a good friend, Philip Bliss (1838–1876), a gospel singer and song writer of great renown.

Bliss wrote the music the night before he and his wife boarded a train for Chicago on December 29, 1876. During a severe snowstorm the train crashed through a bridge over a deep ravine. Bliss escaped but then went back into the train to look for his wife. Neither was ever found.

Always a student of archaeology, Horatio Spafford, his wife, and their new baby daughter settled in Jerusalem in 1881 with a group of friends. They became known as the American colony. After his death in 1888 his family decided to stay, and his daughter, Bertha Spafford Vester, later became a beacon of hope and reconciliation in that troubled land. I knew her personally and considered her a modern saint.

"It Is Well with My Soul" expresses both the reality of trouble and sorrow and the confidence in God to see us through.

When peace like a river attendeth my way,
When sorrows like sea billows roll,
Whatever my lot, Thou hast taught me to say,
"It is well, it is well with my soul."

Refrain
It is well with my soul.
It is well, it is well with my soul.

Though Satan should buffet, tho' trials should come,
Let this blest assurance control,
That Christ hath regarded my helpless estate,
And hath shed His own blood for my soul.

My sin—oh, the bliss of this glorious tho't!
My sin—not in part, but the whole—
Is nailed to His cross and I bear it no more.
Praise the Lord, praise the Lord, O my soul!

And Lord, haste the day when the faith shall be sight,
The clouds be rolled back as a scroll,
The trump shall resound and the Lord shall descend.
"Even so"—it is well with my soul.

Samuel J. Stone (1839–1900)

The Church's One Foundation

In 1863 John Colenso, Anglican bishop of South Africa, wrote a book questioning the accuracy of certain Old Testament writings. This sparked a heated controversy between conservatives and liberals within the church. Colenso's views were considered heresy by many church leaders, including Samuel Stone, an Anglican parish priest in Windsor, England. Stone was a firm believer in the inspiration of Scripture and the need for a personal relationship with Christ. He perceived as heretical such ideas as biblical criticism and the theory of evolution, which were becoming popular at that time. In defense of the traditional faith, Stone wrote "The Church's One Foundation."

The melody was composed by Samuel Sebastian Wesley (1810–1876), grandson of Charles Wesley and a church musician of note. Originally written for another hymn, the tune was matched with Stone's text for use at the Lambeth Conference, a gathering of Anglican bishops from across England, held in 1868.

This hymn has become one of the great hymns of the church. On May 10, 1939, the American Methodist Church was born, bringing together the three major branches of Methodism into one body. As the Declaration of Union was proclaimed, twelve thousand voices united in singing "The Church's One Foundation."

In another arena, the 1941 movie about a small-town minister, "One Foot in Heaven," which starred Fredric March and Martha Scott, ended with the steeple bells ringing out this hymn across the town as a sign of victory and faith. I was technical adviser to that film, and I will never forget the power of this hymn in that final scene.

From a bishops' conference to the organization of a major denomination to a Hollywood movie, "The Church's One Foundation" still stirs and inspires our hearts.

The Church's one Foundation
    Is Jesus Christ, her Lord.

She is His new creation
>By water and the word.
From heav'n He came and sought her
>To be His holy bride;
With His own blood He bought her,
>And for her life He died.

Elect from ev'ry nation,
>Yet one o'er all the earth;
Her charter of salvation,
>One Lord, one faith, one birth;
One holy name she blesses;
>Partakes one holy food;
And to one hope she presses,
>With ev'ry grace endued.

'Mid toil and tribulation,
>And tumult of her war,
She waits the consummation
>Of peace forevermore;
Till, with the vision glorious,
>Her longing eyes are blest,
And the great Church victorious
>Shall be the Church at rest.

Yet she on earth hath union
  With God, the Three in One,
And mystic sweet communion
  With those whose rest is won.
Oh, happy ones and holy!
  Lord, give us grace that we,
Like them, the meek and lowly,
  On high may dwell with Thee.

Will L. Thompson (1847–1909)

Softly and Tenderly

"Softly and Tenderly" was a favorite "invitation" hymn for D. L. Moody and Ira Sankey in their evangelistic crusades. In fact, William J. Reynolds reported in *Songs of Glory* that when Will Thompson visited Moody on his deathbed in 1899, Moody said, "Will, I would rather have written 'Softly and Tenderly, Jesus Is Calling' than anything I have been able to do in my whole life."

Thompson once tried to sell several of his songs for one hundred dollars. When he was turned down he thought, "I'll publish them myself." He did just that, becoming a well-known publisher of popular, patriotic, and sacred music. He also ran a thriving piano and organ business, but it is for his gospel songs that he is best known. Music was always his avocation, and he used to travel by horse and buggy across his home state of Ohio singing his songs. A notebook was his constant companion; ideas for lyrics or tunes would come to him at any time, at any place.

On April 8, 1968, "Softly and Tenderly" was sung by the choir of the Ebenezer Baptist Church in Atlanta, at the memorial service for Dr. Martin Luther King, Jr.

Softly and tenderly Jesus is calling,
Calling for you and for me.
See, on the portals He's waiting and watching,
Watching for you and for me.

Refrain
Come home, come home.
Ye who are weary, come home.
Earnestly, tenderly Jesus is calling,
Calling, "O sinner, come home!"

Why should we tarry when Jesus is pleading,
Pleading for you and for me?
Why should we linger and heed not His mercies,
Mercies for you and for me?

Time is now fleeting; the moments are passing,
Passing from you and from me.
Shadows are gathering; death's night is coming,
Coming for you and for me.

Oh! for the wonderful love He has promised,
Promised for you and for me!
Tho' we have sinned, He has mercy and pardon,
Pardon for you and for me.

Augustus M. Toplady (1740–1778)

Rock of Ages

"Rock of Ages," written as a statement of faith in the midst of theological controversy, has become a favorite of kings and prime ministers as well as common people of all nations. While visiting Ireland at the age of sixteen, its author, Augustus Toplady, was converted at a service held in a barn by an itinerant Wesleyan evangelist named James Morris. For a while Toplady was attracted to the Methodist movement, becoming friends with John and Charles Wesley, but he split with them when he became an ardent believer in the doctrines of John Calvin. As an Anglican priest,

Toplady was a zealous, evangelical preacher, but his running feud with the Wesleys produced some bitter, acrimonious comments. Wesley called him a "chimney sweep" and a "coxcomb." Toplady replied that "John Wesley is guilty of Satanic shamelessness" and often referred to him as "Pope John." The basis of their controversy was the doctrine of predestination and whether perfection can ever be reached in this life.

"Rock of Ages," written in 1776, was Toplady's statement of belief, but today it has such a universal message that the controversy that inspired it has long since been forgotten. Some evidence indicates that Toplady may have taken certain of its phrases from a hymn Charles Wesley had written thirty years earlier. The adversaries were also joined in another way: Toplady was buried in a church built by George Whitfield (a Wesleyan preacher), a church in which John Wesley later preached Whitfield's funeral sermon.

This man who gave us such an enduring legacy in "Rock of Ages" died from tuberculosis at the age of thirty-eight. The hymn's tune was composed in 1830 by a man who dedicated his life to improving church music. He wrote more than one thousand hymn tunes, six hundred original hymn texts, and fifty volumes of church music. Without Thomas Hastings (1784–1872), church music as we know it today would not exist.

Rock of Ages, cleft for me,
Let me hide myself in Thee.
Let the water and the blood,
From Thy wounded side which flowed,
Be of sin the double cure,
Save from wrath and make me pure.

Should my tears forever flow,
Should my zeal no languor know,
These for sin could not atone;
Thou must save, and Thou alone.
In my hand no price I bring;
Simply to Thy cross I cling.

While I draw this fleeting breath,
When my eyes shall close in death,
When I rise to worlds unknown,
And behold Thee on Thy throne,
Rock of Ages, cleft for me,
Let me hide myself in Thee.

Henry van Dyke (1852–1933)

Joyful, Joyful, We Adore Thee

Henry van Dyke was a professor of literature at Princeton University at the time he wrote "Joyful, Joyful, We Adore Thee." As an ordained Presbyterian minister, van Dyke received many invitations to preach. One Sunday he was the guest preacher at Williams College in Massachusetts. At breakfast that morning, he handed a sheet of paper to the president of Williams, with whom he was staying. "Here's a hymn for you," he said. "Your mountains [the Berkshires] were my inspiration. It must be sung to the music of Beethoven's 'Hymn of Joy.'"

Henry van Dyke had a distinguished and varied career. In addition to teaching at Princeton, he pastored the Brick Presbyterian Church in New York City and was moderator of the denomination. He served as a Navy chaplain during World War I and was ambassador to Holland and Luxembourg under President Wilson. He was a prolific writer of devotional books, many of which are still read today.

Ludwig van Beethoven's (1770–1827) "Hymn of Joy," the tune for this hymn, comes out of his last and greatest symphony, the Ninth. It premiered in 1824, Beethoven's last public concert.

By that time he was stone deaf, and at the end of the concert the contralto soloist came down from the stage and turned him around so he could receive the audience's thunderous applause.

A number of hymns have been adapted from Beethoven's works, but "Joyful, Joyful, We Adore Thee" is the most widely used.

Joyful, joyful, we adore Thee,
God of glory, Lord of love;
Hearts unfold like flow'rs before Thee,
Opening to the sun above.
Melt the clouds of sin and sadness;
Drive the dark of doubt away;
Giver of immortal gladness,
Fill us with the light of day!

All Thy works with joy surround Thee;
Earth and heav'n reflect Thy rays;
Stars and angels sing around Thee,
Center of unbroken praise.
Field and forest, vale and mountain,
Flowery meadow, flashing sea,
Chanting bird and flowing fountain
Call us to rejoice in Thee.

Thou art giving and forgiving,
Ever blessing, ever blest,
Wellspring of the joy of living,
Ocean depth of happy rest!
Thou our Father, Christ our Brother—
All who live in love are Thine.
Teach us how to love each other;
Lift us to the joy divine.

Mortals join the mighty chorus
Which the morning stars began.
Father-love is reigning o'er us;
Brother-love binds man to man.
Ever singing, march we onward,
Victors in the midst of strife;
Joyful music leads us sunward
In the triumph song of life.

William W. Walford (1772–1850)

Sweet Hour of Prayer

It was originally thought that "Sweet Hour of Prayer" was written in 1842 by a blind shopkeeper named William Walford who lived in Coleshill, England. The story has it that one day Walford gave a poem he had just written on prayer to his minister who had stopped by the shop to visit him. Three years later this minister, Thomas Salmon, was visiting the United States, where he showed it to the editor of the *New York Observer*. It first appeared in the *Observer* in 1845.

Later research could not verify that a blind William Walford lived in Coleshill around that time, but a Congregational minister with the same name did live in the town of Homerton. This William Walford was the author of many books, one of which was a book on prayer that contained many similarities to the hymn text.

However the text came into being, it was discovered by William Bradbury (1816–1868), eminent composer and piano manufacturer, who composed the tune in 1861. Bradbury's other hymn tunes of note are "The Solid Rock," "He Leadeth Me," "Jesus Loves Me," and "Just as I Am."

Sweet hour of prayer, sweet hour of prayer,
 That calls me from a world of care
And bids me at my Father's throne
 Make all my wants and wishes known!
In seasons of distress and grief
 My soul has often found relief,
And oft escaped the tempter's snare,
 By thy return, sweet hour of prayer.

Sweet hour of prayer, sweet hour of prayer,
 The joy I feel, the bliss I share,
Of those whose anxious spirits burn
 With strong desires for thy return!
With such I hasten to the place
 Where God, my Saviour, shows His face,
And gladly take my station there,
 And wait for thee, sweet hour of prayer.

Sweet hour of prayer, sweet hour of prayer,
 Thy wings shall my petition bear
To Him whose truth and faithfulness
 Engage the waiting soul to bless;
And since He bids me seek His face,
 Believe His word, and trust His grace,

I'll cast on Him my ev'ry care,
    And wait for thee, sweet hour of prayer.

Anna B. Warner (1820–1915)

Jesus Loves Me

Children and new converts the world over sing "Jesus Loves Me," which has been translated into almost every known language. When theologian Karl Barth was asked by a group of students to describe the teachings of Christianity in one sentence, he said, "It is all in the words of a hymn my mother taught me: 'Jesus loves me, this I know, for the Bible tells me so.'"

The words of the hymn appeared in a novel written by Anna and Susan Warner in 1860 entitled *Say and Seal*. In the novel a dying boy asks his friend and Sunday school teacher to sing him a song. "Jesus Loves Me" was that song, written by Anna, who chose to write a new hymn rather than use a familiar one for that scene.

Anna and Susan were well-known authors, writing and collaborating together on seventy books. Susan was probably the best known of the two at the time, but Anna's name lives on through this hymn. The sisters lived near West Point, New York, and each

Sunday held Bible classes in their home for the United States Military Academy cadets. When they died, each was buried with full military honors because of her spiritual service to the men. They left their home to the academy, and it is now a national shrine.

In 1861 William Bradbury (1816–1868), noted for his work in children's music, wrote the tune and added the chorus to the text. The tune is a perfect match for the words and no doubt has aided its popularity over the years.

I well remember learning this hymn from my mother as a young child and singing it in Sunday school as I was growing up. It has never lost its power to touch people's hearts, including my own.

Jesus loves me! this I know
For the Bible tells me so.
Little ones to Him belong;
They are weak but He is strong.

Refrain
Yes, Jesus loves me.
Yes, Jesus loves me.
Yes, Jesus loves me.
The Bible tells me so.

Jesus loves me! loves me still,
Tho' I'm very weak and ill;
That I might from sin be free,
Bled and died upon the tree.

Jesus loves me! He who died,
Heaven's gates to open wide.
He will wash away my sin,
Let His little child come in.

Jesus loves me! He will stay
Close beside me all the way;
Thou hast bled and died for me,
I will henceforth live for Thee.

Isaac Watts (1674–1748)

Isaac Watts was the father of English hymn writing. Before his time there was no congregational singing in England as we know it today. People chanted the psalms in a slow and ponderous manner. When Isaac was eighteen he complained about this to his father, who suggested that Isaac write something better. He did, writing a new hymn every week for the next two years. In 1707 he published a collection of his own hymns, and that volume became the first real hymnbook in the English language.

Watts was born in 1674 in Southampton, England, the oldest of nine children. His father, a deacon in a dissenting Congregational church, was in prison for his nonconformist views when Isaac was born. His mother took the baby with her to visit her husband in prison. Religious dissenters, those who disagreed with the practices of the established church, were routinely persecuted at that time. Dissenting clergy were dismissed from their pulpits, and religious meetings were forbidden. Not until 1689, when Isaac Watts was fifteen years old, was freedom of worship granted.

Though small in stature—five feet tall—with a large head and a long, hooked nose, Watts was a giant in intellect. He wrote volumes of essays, sermons, textbooks, and hymns. He could appeal both to the intellectual and to the child. In fact, his first hymnal was written especially for children. He wrote all his hymns in simple language so that they would be readily understood by the people of his congregations.

Refusing to attend Oxford University because he would not become an Anglican, Watts was ordained in the Reformed Church and served as pastor of an independent church in London. Frail in health most of his life, he spent the last thirty years as an invalid. But his physical problems never affected his mind, and today a monument to his honor stands in Westminster Abbey, the highest honor afforded an English person.

O God, Our Help in Ages Past

Considered to be the finest of Watts's hymns, "O God, Our Help" was originally written as "Our God, Our Help," and the title was later changed by John Wesley. The original version also had nine stanzas. The tune, written by William Croft (1678–1727), one of England's finest musicians, gained recognition only after being sung with Watts's lyrics. J. S. Bach and G. F. Handel both used this tune for one of their works.

O God, our Help in ages past,
Our Hope for years to come,
Our Shelter from the stormy blast,
And our eternal Home!

Under the shadow of Thy throne
Still may we dwell secure;
Sufficient is Thine arm alone,
And our defense is sure.

Before the hills in order stood,
Or earth received her frame,
From everlasting Thou art God,
To endless years the same.

O God, our Help in ages past,
Our Hope for years to come,
Be Thou our Guide while life shall last,
And our eternal Home.

Jesus Shall Reign

"Jesus Shall Reign" is considered the finest missionary hymn
ever written and was one of the first to have a mission emphasis.
Watts must have had a vision of the future, for he wrote it in
1719, well before the missionary movement began to take hold in
England. Many stories have been told about this hymn's influence.
One has it that in 1862 five thousand natives on a South Sea island sang this hymn as a new Christian constitution was installed
by their king.

Jesus shall reign where'er the sun
Does his successive journeys run;

His kingdom spread from shore to shore,
Till moons shall wax and wane no more.

To Him shall endless pray'r be made,
And endless praises crown His head.
His name like sweet perfume shall rise
With ev'ry morning sacrifice.

People and realms of ev'ry tongue
Dwell on His love with sweetest song,
And infant voices shall proclaim
Their early blessings on His name.

Let ev'ry creature rise and bring
His grateful honors to our King;
Angels descend with songs again,
And earth repeat the loud Amen!

I Sing the Mighty Power of God

"I Sing the Mighty Power of God" is one of many hymns
Watts wrote especially for children. In 1715 he wrote a children's
hymnal, the first of its kind in English. Although he was a learned

and literary man, Watts wrote his hymns in a style and language that children could understand.

I sing the mighty pow'r of God,
 That made the mountains rise;
That spread the flowing seas abroad,
 And built the lofty skies.
I sing the wisdom that ordained
 The sun to rule the day;
The moon shines full at His command,
 And all the stars obey.

I sing the goodness of the Lord,
 That filled the earth with food;
He formed the creatures with His word,
 And then pronounced them good.
Lord, how Thy wonders are displayed,
 Where'er I turn my eye:
If I survey the ground I tread,
 Or gaze upon the sky!

There's not a plant or flow'r below,
 But makes Thy glories known;
And clouds arise, and tempests blow,

By order from Thy throne;
While all that borrows life from Thee
    Is ever in Thy care,
And ev'rywhere that man can be,
    Thou, God, art present there.

When I Survey the Wondrous Cross

"When I Survey the Wondrous Cross" represented a new departure in hymn writing. It was based on personal feelings rather than paraphrased Scripture. Such hymns were controversial and represented Watts's willingness to develop new ways to sing praise to God.

This tune was arranged from a Gregorian chant by Lowell Mason (1792–1872), the founder of American church music and a pioneer in establishing music in the public schools.

When I survey the wondrous Cross
On which the Prince of Glory died,
My richest gain I count but loss,
And pour contempt on all my pride.

Forbid it, Lord, that I should boast,
Save in the death of Christ, my God.

All the vain things that charm me most,
I sacrifice them to His blood.

See, from His head, His hands, His feet,
Sorrow and love flow mingled down.
Did e'er such love and sorrow meet,
Or thorns compose so rich a crown?

Were the whole realm of nature mine,
That were a present far too small.
Love so amazing, so divine,
Demands my soul, my life, my all.

Charles Wesley (1707–1788)

More of the hymns of Charles Wesley are being sung today than of any other hymn writer. He took up the mantle from Isaac Watts and brought warmth and feeling to the hymns people sang. Altogether he wrote about sixty-five hundred texts, and it has been said that they had much to do with the growth of the Methodist movement.

Charles's life is inexorably intertwined with that of his brother, John. As students in Oxford they formed a club to deal with a spiritual lethargy they felt existed at the school. Because of their methodical ways they were referred to as "methodists." Ordained as priests in the Anglican Church, they were sent to America in 1736 to help minister in the colony of Georgia. John was chaplain to the colonists and Charles served as personal secretary to Governor James Oglethorpe.

Although that assignment was short-lived and unsuccessful, an experience on board the ship to America would influence their entire lives. They met a group of German Moravians whose faith, evangelical zeal, and enthusiastic hymn singing impressed them. In 1738, back in England, the brothers again were influenced by a group of devout Moravians who operated a mission on Aldersgate Street, London. Realizing that they did not have the joy in their faith or the kind of personal relationship with Christ that the Moravians did, both John and Charles had deep spiritual experiences that changed their lives forever.

The Wesley brothers began to preach and Charles began to write hymns. Because their evangelical zeal was not shared by the Anglican hierarchy and because they were accused of preaching blasphemy, they were denied permission to preach in Anglican churches. Even the church in Epworth, where they had grown up, refused to let them in. That sent them outdoors or into factories, mines, and prisons—anywhere they could attract a crowd. It is said that they worked eighteen hours a day, traveled two hundred fifty thousand miles throughout Great Britain on horseback, and conducted forty thousand public services in a lifetime of ministry. They, and often their converts, were threatened, stoned, hounded, cursed at, and spat upon. William Reynolds, in *Songs of Glory*, writes that in one town, "a crowd was stirred up by the town's leaders and the minister, and surrounded the house where the Wesleys were staying. They broke windows, ripped off shutters, and drove the Wesleys' horses into the pond."

Through it all, Charles wrote hymns. Whitney Dough, in *The Hymn Writers,* says, "If John Wesley was Methodism's head, Charles was its heart." Verse came to him everywhere. Beset by personal tragedy—his beautiful wife, Sarah, was severely scarred from smallpox, and five of his children died in childhood—his hymns spoke of personal faith and God's love. They were forerunners of the gospel song of later years. Some of his best-known and best-loved hymns are the following.

Jesus, Lover of My Soul

Considered to be Wesley's finest hymn, "Jesus, Lover of My Soul" was written in 1738 and has been translated into many languages. When Charles first showed it to his brother, John said it was too sentimental. It was not until after Charles's death in 1788 that it came into general use. Several legends surround its writing. One account sees it as a picture of Wesley's life prior to his conversion. Another relates it to a violent storm at sea while he was returning from America. Whatever the inspiration, it has continued to touch people's hearts down through the ages.

Consider the following story, recounted by William Reynolds in *Songs of Glory:* "Levi Hefner, a Confederate courier, was sent, one night, by his commanding officer, General Robert E. Lee, to take a message through an area partially occupied by Union troops. As he approached a bridge, his horse balked and reared nervously. Hefner dismounted and attempted to calm him. In the darkness, Hefner began singing softly an old, familiar hymn, 'Jesus, Lover of My Soul.' In a few minutes, the horse became quiet. Hefner mounted him, crossed the bridge without incident, and completed his mission.

"A number of years after the war, Hefner attended a reunion of soldiers from both sides. They gathered in small groups to share experiences they remembered from the war. A Union soldier, from Ohio, remembered standing guard one dark night at a bridge. He had been ordered to shoot anyone approaching from the other side. During the night, only one rider came his way, and he raised his rifle to shoot as soon as he could see the form in the darkness. The horse balked, however, and the rider dismounted. To calm the horse, the rider began singing softly an old hymn, 'Jesus, Lover of

My Soul.' The Union soldier told the circle of old soldiers that the sound of the hymn so touched him that he lowered his rifle and quietly turned away. He said, 'I could not shoot him.'

"Levi Hefner jumped up and embraced the Union soldier, saying, 'That was me!' He realized, for the first time, that his singing that dark night had saved his life."

Jesus, Lover of my soul,
    Let me to Thy bosom fly,
While the nearer waters roll,
    While the tempest still is high!
Hide me, O my Saviour, hide,
    Till the storm of life is past.
Safe into the haven guide,
    Oh, receive my soul at last!

Other refuge have I none;
    Hangs my helpless soul on Thee.
Leave, ah, leave me not alone;
    Still support and comfort me!
All my trust on Thee is stayed;
    All my help from Thee I bring.
Cover my defenseless head
    With the shadow of Thy wing.

145

Thou, O Christ, art all I want;
    More than all in Thee I find.
Raise the fallen, cheer the faint,
    Heal the sick, and lead the blind.
Just and holy is Thy name;
    I am all unrighteousness.
False and full of sin I am;
    Thou art full of truth and grace.

Plenteous grace with Thee is found,
    Grace to cover all my sin.
Let the healing streams abound;
    Make and keep me pure within.
Thou of life the Fountain art;
    Freely let me take of Thee.
Spring Thou up within my heart;
    Rise to all eternity.

Christ, the Lord, Is Risen Today

The traditional Easter hymn "Christ, the Lord, Is Risen Today" was originally written without the "alleluia" after each phrase. That word, which means "praise the Lord," was added later so the text would fit the tune. The text was written in 1739 for the first service in the first Wesleyan Chapel, an old iron foundry in London. It was later published in the *Foundry Collection,* one of the sixty-five hymnals Charles compiled.

Christ, the Lord, is risen today, Alleluia!
Sons of men and angels say: Alleluia!
Raise your joys and triumphs high, Alleluia!
Sing, ye heavens, and earth, reply: Alleluia!

Lives again our glorious King, Alleluia!
Where, O death, is now thy sting? Alleluia!
Dying once, He all doth save, Alleluia!
Where thy victory, O grave? Alleluia!

Love's redeeming work is done, Alleluia!
Fought the fight, the battle won, Alleluia!
Death in vain forbids Him rise, Alleluia!
Christ has opened Paradise, Alleluia!

Soar we now where Christ has led, Alleluia!
Following our exalted Head, Alleluia!
Made like Him, like Him we rise, Alleluia!
Ours the cross, the grave, the skies, Alleluia!

Hail the Lord of earth and heaven! Alleluia!
Praise to thee by both be given, Alleluia!
Thee we greet triumphant now, Alleluia!
Hail, the Resurrection thou! Alleluia!

O For a Thousand Tongues

Charles Wesley wrote "O For a Thousand Tongues" in 1739 to commemorate the first anniversary of his conversion. It was inspired by a chance remark by Moravian leader Peter Bohler, who said, "Had I a thousand tongues, I would praise Jesus Christ with all of them."

Originally written with nineteen stanzas, the hymn includes only six today.

O for a thousand tongues to sing
My great Redeemer's praise,
The glories of my God and King,
The triumphs of His grace.

My gracious Master and my God,
Assist me to proclaim,

To spread thro' all the earth abroad,
The honors of Thy name.

Jesus! the name that charms our fears,
That bids our sorrows cease;
'Tis music in the sinner's ears,
'Tis life, and health, and peace.

He breaks the power of canceled sin,
He sets the prisoner free;
His blood can make the foulest clean;
His blood availed for me.

Hear Him, ye deaf; His praise, ye dumb,
Your loosened tongues employ;
Ye blind, behold your Saviour come;
And leap, ye lame, for joy.

Hark! the Herald Angels Sing

Written less than a year after his conversion at Aldersgate,
"Hark! the Herald Angels Sing" reflects Wesley's newfound spiri-

tual experience. It is the most popular of his eighteen Christmas hymns, in part because of its tune. For more than one hundred years it was sung to the tune of "Christ the Lord Is Risen Today," but in 1856 William Cummings, an English musician, adapted a melody from a choral work that Felix Mendelssohn had written in 1840. This tune was the perfect match for Wesley's text, as evidenced by the hymn's popularity over the years.

> Hark! the herald angels sing,
> "Glory to the newborn King;
> Peace on earth, and mercy mild;
> God and sinners reconciled."
> Joyful, all ye nations, rise,
> Join the triumph of the skies;
> With th' angelic hosts proclaim,
> "Christ is born in Bethlehem."
> Hark! the herald angels sing,
> "Glory to the newborn King."
>
> Christ, by highest heaven adored;
> Christ, the everlasting Lord:
> Late in time behold Him come,
> Offspring of a virgin's womb.
> Veiled in flesh the Godhead see,

Hail th' incarnate Deity!
Pleased as man with men t'appear,
Jesus our Immanuel here.
Hark! the herald angels sing,
"Glory to the newborn King."

Hail the heaven-born Prince of Peace!
Hail the Sun of righteousness!
Light and life to all He brings,
Risen with healing in His wings:
Mild He lays His glory by,
Born that man no more may die;
Born to raise the sons of earth;
Born to give them second birth.
Hark! the herald angels sing,
"Glory to the newborn King."

Come, Desire of nations, come!
Fix in us Thy humble home:
Rise, the woman's conquering seed,
Bruise in us the serpent's head;
Adam's likeness now efface,
Stamp thine image in its place:
Second Adam from above,

Reinstate us in Thy love.
Hark! the herald angels sing,
"Glory to the newborn King."

Love Divine, All Loves Excelling

First published in 1747, "Love Divine, All Loves Excelling" was one of the first hymns on the theme that God is love, a concept preached by the Wesleys. They believed that God offered salvation to all people, not just a select few, as the Calvinists taught.

The tune was composed by John Zundel (1815–1882), organist of the Plymouth Congregational Church in Brooklyn, New York, where Henry Ward Beecher was pastor. Zundel and Beecher compiled an unusual hymnal in 1855, probably the first to put both words and music on the same page.

Love Divine, all loves excelling,
    Joy of heav'n, to earth come down!
Fix in us Thy humble dwelling;
    All Thy faithful mercies crown.
Jesus, Thou art all compassion;
    Pure, unbounded love Thou art.

Visit us with Thy salvation;
 Enter ev'ry trembling heart.

Breathe, oh, breathe Thy loving Spirit
 Into ev'ry troubled breast!
Let us all in Thee inherit;
 Let us find that second rest.
Take away our bent to sinning;
 Alpha and Omega be.
End of faith, as its Beginning,
 Set our hearts at liberty.

Come, Almighty to Deliver;
 Let us all Thy life receive.
Suddenly return, and never,
 Nevermore Thy temples leave.
Thee we would be always blessing,
 Serve Thee as Thy hosts above,
Pray, and praise Thee without ceasing,
 Glory in Thy perfect love.

Finish then Thy new creation;
 Pure and spotless let us be.
Let us see Thy great salvation,

Perfectly restored in Thee:
Changed from glory into glory,
    Till in heav'n we take our place,
Till we cast our crowns before Thee,
    Lost in wonder, love, and praise.

John Greenleaf Whittier (1807–1892)

Dear Lord and Father of Mankind

John Greenleaf Whittier was one of America's most beloved and respected writers. In fact, many called him our country's greatest poet. Unlike other literary giants of his day—Ralph Waldo Emerson, Henry Wadsworth Longfellow, James Russell Lowell, and Oliver Wendell Holmes—Whittier had little education or formal training. He grew up on a farm in New Hampshire and as a teenager developed a love for poetry through reading the words of Scottish poet Robert Burns. By the age of twenty-five he had already been published and his poetry had begun to attract literary attention.

Whittier was a lifelong Quaker in his beliefs, speech, and lifestyle. He believed in simplicity, genuine piety, and faith that was reflected in a person's attitudes and deeds toward others. He never wrote hymns as such, for hymn singing was not part of Quaker worship, but his poems have been the source of at least seventy-five hymn texts.

Whittier was appalled by the emotionalism of the revival meetings common in his day. He thought emotion in worship was an affront to God and a false way to help people find God. In 1872 one of his poems, entitled "The Brewing of Soma," was published in the *Atlantic Monthly*. In it Whittier compared revivals and camp meetings to the intoxicating beverage, *soma,* that Hindu priests used during their worship. That drink produced a "frenzy, a sacred madness, an ecstatic storm of drunken joy." Whittier then described true Christian worship, and it is this latter portion of his poem that became the text for "Dear Lord and Father of Mankind." It is in quietness and calmness that we can find true worship. The tune is by an Irish composer, Frederick Maker (1844–1927), who also wrote the tune for "Beneath the Cross of Jesus."

In spite of his lack of formal education, Whittier had an extensive career in journalism. He also served in the Massachusetts state legislature and was the first person to suggest the formation of the Republican Party. Next to his writing, he was best known for his efforts to abolish slavery. He was a man of and for the people, and his poetry reflects both his roots on the land and the genuineness of his life. He made a vital contribution both to our literary and religious life.

Dear Lord and Father of mankind,
    Forgive our foolish ways!
Reclothe us in our rightful mind;
    In purer lives Thy service find;
In deeper rev'rence, praise.

In simple trust like theirs who heard,
    Beside the Syrian sea,
The gracious calling of the Lord,
    Let us, like them, without a word,
Rise up and follow Thee.

Drop Thy still dews of quietness
    Till all our strivings cease.
Take from our souls the strain and stress,
    And let our ordered lives confess
The beauty of thy peace.

Breathe thro' the heats of our desire
    Thy coolness and Thy balm.
Let sense be dumb, let flesh retire;
    Speak thro' the earthquake, wind, and fire,
O still small voice of calm!

William Williams (1717–1791)

Guide Me, O Thou Great Jehovah

Imagine riding on horseback across your country, preaching in small towns, holding revivals, and, wherever you went, singing the great hymns of your land, many of which you yourself wrote. Such was the life of William Williams in his native Wales. It is estimated that he covered nearly one hundred thousand miles in his forty-three years as an itinerant evangelist. He traveled through rain and snow, in daylight and at night, often attacked by gangs and robbers.

Williams didn't start out to be a preacher, however. He was studying to be a doctor when he heard a sermon by Welsh evangelist Howell Harris that changed his life. Through that experience he believed God was calling him to the ministry. He was ordained an Anglican priest but soon left that church because his evangelical views were in conflict with Anglican leaders. Then began his life's real ministry.

Although Williams was an effective preacher, his great strength lay in his music. He wrote more than eight hundred hymns in Welsh, most of which have never been translated, but in Wales they are well known and often used to teach illiterate people to read.

"Guide Me, O Thou Great Jehovah," his finest hymn, first appeared in a hymnal published in 1745. The imagery compares the journey of the Israelites to the Promised Land with the way we should live the Christian life. God will guide, protect, and strengthen as we "pilgrim through a barren land."

The tune for this hymn was written by John Hughes (1873–1932), a noted Welsh composer, on the occasion of a singing festival in Wales. Although it was written almost two hundred fifty years ago, the hymn remains one of that country's most popular.

Guide me, O Thou great Jehovah,
    Pilgrim through this barren land.
I am weak, but Thou art mighty;
    Hold me with Thy powerful hand.
Bread of Heaven, Bread of Heaven,
    Feed me till I want no more
Feed me till I want no more.

Open now the crystal fountain,
    Whence the healing stream doth flow;
Let the fire and cloudy pillar

Lead me all my journey through.
Strong Deliv'rer, strong Deliv'rer,
Be Thou still my Strength and Shield
Be Thou still my Strength and Shield.

When I tread the verge of Jordan,
Bid my anxious fears subside;
Death of death, and hell's destruction,
Land me safe on Canaan's side.
Songs of praises, songs of praises
I will ever give to Thee,
I will ever give to Thee.

Acknowledgments

For her extensive and thorough research and her care for the accuracy of this text, I appreciate the work of my daughter, Margaret Peale Everett. She also was very helpful in selecting the hymns. Her comment to me was, "I have loved most of these hymns all of my life."

I am grateful to Sybil Light, my competent secretary, for her efficient and thoughtful handling of all the work involved in this manuscript.

While I have consulted many sources for the information contained in this book, the following have been particularly helpful:

Dough, Whitney J. *The Hymn Writers*. Orlando: Messages, 1983.

McKim, Lindajo H. *The Presbyterian Hymnal Companion*. Louisville: Westminster/John Knox Press, 1993.

Osbeck, Kenneth W. *101 Hymn Stories*. Grand Rapids: Kregel Publications, 1982.

Osbeck, Kenneth W. *101 More Hymn Stories*. Grand Rapids: Kregel Publications, 1985.

Reynolds, William J. *Songs of Glory*. Grand Rapids: Zondervan, 1990.

Index of Hymn Titles

A Mighty Fortress Is Our God
73
Abide with Me   77
All Hail the Power of Jesus' Name
97
All the Way My Saviour Leads Me
29
Amazing Grace   91
America the Beautiful   10

Battle Hymn of the Republic   66
Blessed Assurance   32
Blest Be the Tie That Binds   43
Break Thou the Bread of Life   72

Christ, the Lord, Is Risen Today
146

Day Is Dying in the West   71
Dear Lord and Father of Mankind
154

Faith of Our Fathers   40

God of Grace   46
God of Our Fathers   106
God Will Take Care of You   80
Guide Me, O Thou Great Jehovah
157

Hark! the Herald Angels Sing   149
Have Thine Own Way, Lord   100
He Leadeth Me   48
Holy, Holy, Holy   59
How Great Thou Art   62

I Love Thy Kingdom, Lord   33
I Need Thee Every Hour   57
I Sing the Mighty Power of God   138
In the Garden   85
It Came upon the Midnight Clear   111
It Is Well with My Soul   116

Jesus Calls Us   4
Jesus Loves Me   132
Jesus, Lover of My Soul   143
Jesus, Saviour, Pilot Me   64
Jesus Shall Reign   137
Jesus, the Very Thought of Thee   25
Joyful, Joyful, We Adore Thee   127
Just as I Am   37

Love Divine, All Loves Excelling   152

More Love to Thee   103
My Faith Looks Up to Thee   94
My Country, 'Tis of Thee   114

Nearer, My God, to Thee   1

O For a Thousand Tongues   148
O God, Our Help in Ages Past   136
O Little Town of Bethlehem   19
O Love That Wilt Not Let Me Go   82
O Master, Let Me Walk with Thee   51
Onward, Christian Soldiers   7

Rock of Ages   124

Silent Night, Holy Night   88
Softly and Tenderly   122
Spirit of God, Descend upon My Heart   26
Sweet By and By   17
Sweet Hour of Prayer   130

Take My Life   54
The Church's One Foundation   119
The Old Rugged Cross   14

There's a Wideness in God's Mercy
  41

What a Friend We Have in Jesus
  108
When I Survey the Wondrous
  Cross   *140*
When Morning Gilds the Skies
  23

Index of First Lines of Hymns

A mighty Fortress is our God, 75

Abide with me! Fast falls the eventide. 79

All hail the pow'r of Jesus' name! 99

All the way my Saviour leads me. 30

Amazing grace! how sweet the sound! 93

Be not dismayed whate'er betide; 81

Blessed assurance, Jesus is mine! 32

Blest be the tie that binds 45

Break Thou the bread of life 72

Christ, the Lord, is risen today, Alleluia! 147

Day is dying in the West, 71

Dear Lord and Father of mankind, 156

Faith of our fathers, living still 40

God of grace and God of glory, 47

God of our fathers, whose almighty hand 107

Guide me, O Thou great Jehovah, *158*

Hark! the herald angels sing, *150*
Have Thine own way, Lord! *101*
He leadeth me! Oh, blessed tho't! *50*
Holy, Holy, Holy, Lord God Almighty! *60*

I come to the garden alone, *87*
I love Thy kingdom, Lord, *35*
I need Thee ev'ry hour, *58*
I sing the mighty pow'r of God, *139*
It came upon the midnight clear, *112*

Jesus calls us; o'er the tumult *5*
Jesus, Lover of my soul, *145*
Jesus loves me! this I know *133*
Jesus, Saviour, pilot me *65*
Jesus shall reign where'er the sun *137*
Jesus, the very thought of Thee *25*

Joyful, joyful, we adore Thee, *128*
Just as I am, without one plea *38*

Love Divine, all loves excelling, *152*

Mine eyes have seen the glory *68*
More love to Thee, O Christ, *104*
My country, 'tis of thee, *115*
My faith looks up to Thee, *95*

Nearer, my God, to Thee, *2*

O beautiful for spacious skies, *12*
O for a thousand tongues to sing *148*
O God, our Help in ages past, *136*
O little town of Bethlehem, *21*
O Lord, my God! When I in awesome wonder *63*

O Love that wilt not let me go, *83*

O Master, let me walk with Thee *53*

On a hill far away stood an old rugged Cross, *15*

Onward, Christian soldiers! *8*

Rock of Ages, cleft for me, *126*

Silent night, holy night, *90*

Softly and tenderly Jesus is calling, *123*

Spirit of God, descend upon my heart. *27*

Sweet hour of prayer, sweet hour of prayer, *131*

Take my life, and let it be *55*

The Church's one Foundation *120*

There's a land that is fairer than day, *18*

There's a wideness in God's mercy *42*

What a Friend we have in Jesus, *109*

When I survey the wondrous Cross *140*

When morning gilds the skies, *24*

When peace like a river attendeth my way, *118*

Topical Index of Hymns

Assurance

All the Way My Saviour Leads Me
  29
Amazing Grace   91
Blessed Assurance   32
God Will Take Care of You   80
He Leadeth Me   48
It Is Well with My Soul   116
O God, Our Help in Ages Past
  136

Children

Jesus Loves Me   132
Onward, Christian Soldiers   7

Christmas

Hark! the Herald Angels Sing
  149
It Came upon the Midnight Clear
  111
O Little Town of Bethlehem   19
Silent Night, Holy Night   88

The Church

A Mighty Fortress Is Our God
  73
Blest Be the Tie That Binds   43
Faith of Our Fathers   40
I Love Thy Kingdom, Lord   33

O God, Our Help in Ages Past
    136
Onward, Christian Soldiers   7
The Church's One Foundation
    119

Comfort

A Mighty Fortress Is Our God
    73
Abide with Me   77
God Will Take Care of You   80
Guide Me, O Thou Great Jehovah
    157
I Need Thee Every Hour   57
Jesus, Lover of My Soul   143
My Faith Looks Up to Thee   94
Nearer, My God, to Thee   1
O God, Our Help in Ages Past
    136
O Love That Wilt Not Let Me Go
    82
Rock of Ages   124
What a Friend We Have in Jesus
    108

Commitment

God of Grace   46
Have Thine Own Way, Lord   100
Jesus Calls Us   4
O Love That Wilt Not Let Me Go
    82
O Master, Let Me Walk with Thee
    51
Spirit of God, Descend upon My
    Heart   26
Take My Life   54

Communion

Break Thou the Bread of Life   72
When I Survey the Wondrous
    Cross   140

The Cross

Rock of Ages   124
The Old Rugged Cross   14
When I Survey the Wondrous
    Cross   140

Devotion

Abide with Me   77

Guide Me, O Thou Great Jehovah
   157

How Great Thou Art   62

In the Garden   85

It Is Well with My Soul   116

Jesus, Lover of My Soul   143

Jesus, the Very Thought of Thee
   25

More Love to Thee   103

My Faith Looks Up to Thee   94

Nearer, My God, to Thee   1

O Love That Wilt Not Let Me Go
   82

O Master, Let Me Walk with Thee
   51

What a Friend We Have in Jesus
   108

Easter

Christ, the Lord, Is Risen Today
   146

Evening

Day Is Dying in the West   71

Guidance

All the Way My Saviour Leads Me
   29

God Will Take Care of You   80

Guide Me, O Thou Great Jehovah
   157

He Leadeth Me   48

Jesus, Saviour, Pilot Me   64

My Faith Looks Up to Thee   94

O God, Our Help in Ages Past
   136

Heaven

Sweet By and By   17

My Faith Looks Up to Thee   94

The Holy Spirit

Spirit of God, Descend upon My
   Heart   26

Invitation

Jesus Calls Us   4
Just as I Am   37
Softly and Tenderly   122

Missions and Evangelism

All Hail the Power of Jesus' Name   97
Jesus Calls Us   4
Faith of Our Fathers   40
Jesus Shall Reign   137
O For a Thousand Tongues   148
Take My Life   54
The Church's One Foundation   119

Patriotic

America the Beautiful   10
Battle Hymn of the Republic   66
God of Our Fathers   106
My Country, 'Tis of Thee   114

Praise

A Mighty Fortress Is Our God   73
All Hail the Power of Jesus' Name   97
Amazing Grace   91
Blessed Assurance   32
Holy, Holy, Holy   59
How Great Thou Art   62
I Sing the Mighty Power of God   138
Jesus Shall Reign   137
Jesus, the Very Thought of Thee   25
Joyful, Joyful, We Adore Thee   127
Love Divine, All Loves Excelling   152
O For a Thousand Tongues   148
O God, Our Help in Ages Past   136
When Morning Gilds the Skies   23

Prayer

Dear Lord and Father of Mankind
   154

I Need Thee Every Hour   *57*

In the Garden   *85*

Sweet Hour of Prayer   *130*

What a Friend We Have in Jesus
   108

Worship

A Mighty Fortress Is Our God
   73

All Hail the Power of Jesus' Name
   97

Dear Lord and Father of Mankind
   154

Holy, Holy, Holy   *59*

How Great Thou Art   *62*

Jesus Shall Reign   *137*

Joyful, Joyful, We Adore Thee
   127

Love Divine, All Loves Excelling
   152

O For a Thousand Tongues   *148*

O God, Our Help in Ages Past
   136

There's a Wideness in God's Mercy
   41